MW01048034

The Minneapolis Regional Chamber of Commerce and Community Communications, Inc.
would like to express our gratitude to these companies for their leadership in the development of this book.

Allianz

A‐UGSBURG
C O L L E G E

MALL OF AMERICA.

PRICEWATERHOUSECOOPERS

TWIN CITIES

Heart of the Lakes, Star of the North

By *Craig McNamara*

Corporate Profiles by *Barb Ernster*

Featuring the Photography of *Conrad Bloomquist*

TWIN CITIES

Heart of the Lakes, Star of the North

By Craig McNamara
Corporate Profiles by Barbara Ernster
Featuring the photography of Conrad Bloomquist

Produced in cooperation with
the Minneapolis Regional Chamber of Commerce

Ronald P. Beers, *Publisher*

Staff for *Twin Cities: Heart of the Lakes, Star of the North*
Acquisitions: Henry S. Beers
Publisher's Sales Associates: Susan Adams, Henry Hintermeister,
Rickey Heaton and Jody Karow
Editor in Chief: Wendi L. Lewis
Profile Editor: Mary Catherine Phillips
Design Director: Scott Phillips
Designer: Robert Galerno
Photo Editors: Wendi L. Lewis and Robert Galerno
Production Manager: Christi Stevens
Accounting Services: Stephanie Perez
Pre-press/Color Separations: Artcraft Graphic Productions
Print Production: Walsworth Publishing Company

CCI

Community Communications, Inc.
Montgomery, Alabama

Leonard J. Jagoda, *Chief Executive Officer*
Ronald P. Beers, *President*
W. David Brown, *Chief Operating Officer*

© 2002 Community Communications
All Rights Reserved
Published 2002
First Edition
ISBN Number: 1-58192-063-6

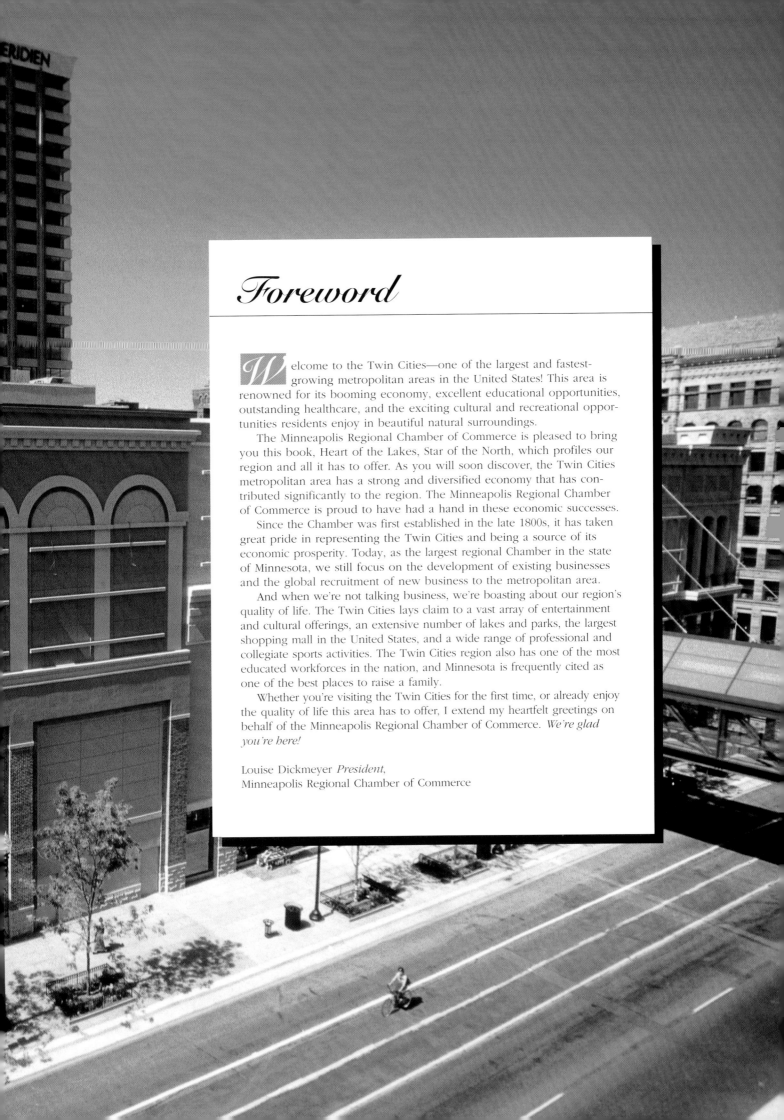

Foreword

Welcome to the Twin Cities—one of the largest and fastest-growing metropolitan areas in the United States! This area is renowned for its booming economy, excellent educational opportunities, outstanding healthcare, and the exciting cultural and recreational opportunities residents enjoy in beautiful natural surroundings.

The Minneapolis Regional Chamber of Commerce is pleased to bring you this book, Heart of the Lakes, Star of the North, which profiles our region and all it has to offer. As you will soon discover, the Twin Cities metropolitan area has a strong and diversified economy that has contributed significantly to the region. The Minneapolis Regional Chamber of Commerce is proud to have had a hand in these economic successes.

Since the Chamber was first established in the late 1800s, it has taken great pride in representing the Twin Cities and being a source of its economic prosperity. Today, as the largest regional Chamber in the state of Minnesota, we still focus on the development of existing businesses and the global recruitment of new business to the metropolitan area.

And when we're not talking business, we're boasting about our region's quality of life. The Twin Cities lays claim to a vast array of entertainment and cultural offerings, an extensive number of lakes and parks, the largest shopping mall in the United States, and a wide range of professional and collegiate sports activities. The Twin Cities region also has one of the most educated workforces in the nation, and Minnesota is frequently cited as one of the best places to raise a family.

Whether you're visiting the Twin Cities for the first time, or already enjoy the quality of life this area has to offer, I extend my heartfelt greetings on behalf of the Minneapolis Regional Chamber of Commerce. *We're glad you're here!*

Louise Dickmeyer *President,*
Minneapolis Regional Chamber of Commerce

Preface

For Sharon, Matthew and Michael

When I was growing up in St. Paul, trips to downtown Minneapolis meant just one thing: another visit to the dentist. I never minded, though, and it wasn't only because I was getting a day out of school. From the dentist's chair, I could look directly onto the Foshay Tower across the street. That view of Minneapolis's tallest skyscraper made every cavity seem almost worth it, even if I was only seeing the tower's midsection.

Over the years, I've lost none of my fascination for the Foshay, even as taller, showier buildings have sprung up around it. But that fascination, I realize now, was only skin deep. Sure, I loved it for its Washington Monument-style profile and the big block letters at it's peak that glowed FOSHAY at night, but there's more to its significance than that.

I didn't know, for instance, that Wilbur Foshay was a utilities baron who built the tower for the lavish headquarters of his nation-spanning empire. Or that, incredibly, only two months after its gala opening, the stock market crash of 1929 destroyed Foshay's empire and Foshay himself soon went to prison due to financial improprieties.

Discoveries like that have made working on this book so interesting. I went from a surface knowledge of the Twin Cities to a deeper under-standing of the historical, economic, and social forces that have shaped, and continue to shape Minneapolis and St. Paul. Whether you're a lifelong resident or a newcomer, I hope I can bring to light information or a new perspective that fascinates you as well.

Craig McNamara
Author

Part 1

CITY of LAKES

When the new skyscraper for Norwest Bank (now Wells Fargo Bank) was in the planning stages, it was obvious even then that this would be a tower of grace and grandeur, one of the defining buildings of the Minneapolis skyline. The design by renowned architect Cesar Pelli was a multi-tiered homage to the art deco era of architecture and a striking change from the stodgy, boxy look of the fourteen-story building that had occupied the site until it was destroyed by fire in 1982.

But perhaps more significantly, it would rise to a height slightly above that of its neighbor to the south, eclipsing the IDS Center's claim as Minneapolis's tallest building. However, by the time construction was completed, the Norwest Center had shrunk to three feet shy of being the new record-holder. Mr. Pelli and bank executives, after additional thought, had decided that that sort of one-upmanship was not in keeping with the spirit of Minneapolis.

Ambitious yet humble. Competitive yet considerate of others. Forward-thinking in so many ways, but always respectful of the traditions of the past. These are the qualities you'll find in the people, the companies, and the institutions that make up Minneapolis today.

(Above) Within its borders, Minneapolis boasts some of the most beautiful inner city lakes in the world.

From its beginnings as a flour and lumber milling town on the banks of the Mississippi more than 150 years ago, the city has grown to more than 368,000 residents spread over 58.7 square miles. Within its borders you'll find vibrant neighborhoods of all income levels, plus quaint shopping corners, live theatres and entertainment venues, universities, and some of the most beautiful inner city lakes in the world. Although primarily settled by Scandinavians, Minneapolis has become a city of great diversity, in both its citizenry and the ethnic traditions that are commemorated and celebrated.

The downtown area is particularly impressive, avoiding the obsolescence that troubles many other cities' central business districts. Retail remains strong and the skyline is ever-changing, as the skyscrapers of new corporate headquarters carefully integrate with the historic architecture of

(Left) From its beginnings as a flour and lumber milling town on the banks of the Mississippi River more than 150 years ago, Minneapolis has grown to over 368,000 residents spread over 58.7 square miles.

Minnesota's four distinct seasons are often cited as one of the state's most compelling characteristics.

A CITY ESTABLISHED BY THE SHORE

ppropriately, the City of Lakes began with water. Not a lake, however, but the Mississippi River, and a curtain of waterfalls just off the shore of what was destined to become downtown Minneapolis. By the late seventeenth century, the area around these falls was held by France and occupied mainly by the Souix family of tribes. Father Louis Hennepin, a French explorer making his way through the territory, came upon the falls in 1680, which he named The Falls of St. Anthony in honor of his patron saint. Though the coming century would see control of the territory pass from the French to the British and finally to the new United States, the name would stick, popularized in Hennepin's published descriptions of his journey.

By the end of the Revolutionary War, the new United States' western border extended to the Mississippi River. To maintain an American presence along the edge of this frontier, President Thomas Jefferson dispatched the first American military expedition, led by Zebulon Pike, to scout locations for permanent garrisons along the Mississippi. Reaching the point where the Mississippi and Minnesota Rivers meet, Pike negotiated with the Souix to purchase the site for the establishment of Fort Snelling on the high bluffs overlooking the

(Above) Minneapolis and St. Anthony were linked by a suspension bridge in 1854, one of the first bridges constructed across the Mississippi. The two towns remained in fierce competition until, by 1864, the population of Minneapolis far surpassed its sister and St. Anthony was absorbed by an act of the State Legislature in 1872. Pictured is a view of St. Anthony and Minneapolis from the Winslow House showing Main Street in St. Anthony, Hennepin Island, and South Minneapolis, 1857. Photo by Benjamin Franklin Upton, courtesy Minnesota Historical Society

(Left) With unlimited water power and a river to transport trees from Minnesota's lush forests up north, the conditions along the St. Anthony Falls were ideal for establishing a new lumber industry. Pictured, St Anthony Falls and Pioneer Lumber Mill, Minneapolis ca. 1860. Photo by Benjamin Franklin Upton, courtesy Minnesota Historical Society

river valley. Just as significantly, the purchase also included nine miles of land along both sides of the Mississippi, north to the Falls of St. Anthony. The intention was to secure the fort a vital source of waterpower for sawing logs and grinding flour, but, inevitably, the falls proved irresistible to settlers in the area as well. Though the swift, shallow water below the St. Anthony cataract prohibited the steamboat access that was

In the late 1800s, Minneapolis was manufacturing two million barrels of flour annually, displacing St. Louis as the nation's leading flour center and earning its first nickname, "The Mill City." Pictured is a general view of flour mills along the canal, Minneapolis, with train; ca. 1890. Photo courtesy Minnesota Historical Society

making the fledgling community of St. Paul an important commercial center a few miles downriver, here the pioneers found the flatter land, with a mix of forests and prairie, was easier to develop than St. Paul's more rugged topography. And with both unlimited water power and a river to transport trees from Minnesota's lush forests up north, the conditions were ideal for establishing a new lumber industry.

The falls' first private sawmill was built in 1837, by Franklin Steele, a storekeeper from Fort Snelling. That was the beginning of a small boom in development that would coalesce into the village of St. Anthony on the river's east bank. Though private enterprise was technically illegal, that didn't stop ambitious pioneers from making claims on any undeveloped land near the falls.

Steele's bookkeeper, John Stevens, went so far as to strike a deal with the government in 1850 for 160 acres on the west bank of the falls; in exchange, he would operate a free ferry service for Fort Snelling troops. Stevens' house became the first structure in the sister settlement forming across the river from St. Anthony. The claims of the squatters were eventually recognized as the military withdrew from the falls, and, in 1855, the entire west bank was opened for settlement. A year later, the community was incorporated as Minneapolis—a name suggested by local school teacher Charles Hoag, who combined the Indian word for water, Minne, with polis, the Greek word for city.

Minneapolis and St. Anthony were linked by a suspension bridge in 1854, one of the first bridges constructed across the Mississippi. However, despite this physical connection and growing social and economic ties, the towns remained in fierce competition, not only for power from the falls, but for the lumber and grain milling business it made possible. In 1867, a pair of dams would be constructed at the falls to ensure enough power for everyone, but within five years, the rivalry would be all but over. From about 300 people in 1854, Minneapolis had swelled to 4,600 a little more than a decade later. In recognition of its greater growth and prosperity, Minneapolis finally absorbed St. Anthony by an act of the state legislature in 1872.

After a downturn during the Civil War years, the lumber business nearly doubled its production during the 1870s. Minneapolis became the world's leading lumber market by 1899; however, its dominance was short-lived. As lumber companies exhausted the northern Minnesota forests and turned elsewhere, flour milling moved to the forefront as Minneapolis' largest industry.

As farmers arriving in the 1850s had discovered, spring wheat was the only practical crop for Minnesota's tough prairie soil. Over the next several decades, amber fields of grain would cover the Midwestern landscape, supplying an ever-growing number of flour mills. With the increasing output made possible by new farming machinery, abundant water power, and Minnesota's growing network of rail connections, conditions were right for Minneapolis to become a major flour-milling center—if a more effective way could be found to grind Minnesota's wheat into flour. The problem was that the brittle, outer layer of spring wheat left behind a brown residue when ground by the mills. This made the flour look impure and limited its appeal beyond the local market.

Knowing that success depended on shipping flour around the country, millers like Cadwallader Washburn struggled to find a better way of processing the flour. Eventually, Washburn's partner, George Christian, devised a machine with Edmund LaCroix that used compressed air to blow away the outer coating as the grains were cracked, making it possible to grind a fine white flour that was actually higher in nutritional value than competing flours. Washburn's flour became an overnight success. Additional improvements in the milling process, made by Washburn's later partner, John Crosby, made the business even more profitable. Washburn constructed a six-story mill on the west bank of the river, the largest flour mill in the United States west of Buffalo, and was turning out 840 barrels a day.

Other area millers, adopting the Washburn-Crosby Company's techniques, found similar demand for their product. Around this time, Minneapolis' second great milling

John Pillsbury recognized the potential of the new flour industry in Minneapolis, and, starting with the purchase of one old mill, he and his nephew, Charles, were able to form their own company by 1874. Pictured are the Pillsbury Flour Mills, Minneapolis ca. 1920. Photo by Ewing Galloway, courtesy Minnesota Historical Society

firm was established by the Pillsbury family. At first glance, John Pillsbury may not have seemed like a likely contender— his previous business, a hardware store, had gone bankrupt, leaving him with debts that took six years to repay—but by then the flour business in the Twin Cities was booming, and Pillsbury knew a good opportunity when he saw it. With his nephew, Charles, he invested in a rundown flour mill, running the business so successfully that they were able to form their own company in 1874. Six years later, eight of the twenty-five flour mills in Minneapolis were owned by either the Pillsbury family or the Washburn-Crosby Company. Together, the two millers were providing more than half of the Minneapolis output. Minneapolis' flours became America's premium flours, fetching 10 to 20 percent more in price than other markets' flours. Minneapolis was manufacturing two million barrels of flour annually, displacing St. Louis as the nation's leading flour center and earning its first nickname, "The Mill City."

With a confidence and economic means brought on by lumber and flour mills, Minneapolis as we know it today began to take shape. Over the next two decades, public and private buildings went up at an unprecedented rate—massive, ornate buildings, many of which are still standing today. A new city hall rose up at the intersection of Third Avenue and

A new city hall rose up at the intersection of Third Avenue and Fifth Street, with a clock tower that made it the tallest structure in Minneapolis. Pictured, a man works on the mechanism of the courthouse tower clock, ca. 1900. Photo by Minneapolis Journal, courtesy Minnesota Historical Society

The first skyscraper west of the Mississippi was the 12-story Metropolitan Life Insurance Building, with its lavish interior of glass, marble, and wrought iron. The building was demolished in 1961. Pictured is the Metropolitan Life Insurance Building, Third Street and Second Avenue, Minneapolis, 1911. Photo by Charles J. Hibbard, courtesy Minneapolis Historical Society

Fifth Street, with a clock tower that made it the tallest structure in Minneapolis. And the first skyscraper west of the Mississippi was built, the twelve-story Metropolitan Life Insurance Building, with its lavish interior of glass, marble, and wrought iron (sadly, demolished in the name of urban renewal in 1961).

As it expanded skyward, the city grew geographically as well, reaching every direction from the riverbank. For the next thirty years, Minneapolis's size would increase to the boundaries that have remained largely unchanged ever since. Population soared, reaching more than 190,000 by the turn of the century.

The 1880s also saw a shift in the location of downtown's center. Stores and shops had originally concentrated near the base of the St. Anthony Falls' suspension bridge, establishing Minneapolis' early central business district. But the expansion of the street grid and streetcar lines moved businesses south along Hennepin and Nicollet Avenues and ended the concentration of Minneapolis along the riverfront.

But Minneapolis wasn't just pulling away from the shoreline. Gradually, it was reducing its dependence on the river's flour and timber industries and diversifying its economic base for the coming century. ∎

Outside shot of Minneapolis City Hall and Hennepin County Courthouse,
1903. Photo courtesy Minneapolis Historical Society

3

A FIRM FOUNDATION

any of Minneapolis' current industries owe at least part of their existence to the one great business that didn't survive. Though the lumber industry thrived only a brief period in Minneapolis' history, the long-term effects of its presence were felt throughout Minnesota's economy for years to come.

Thanks to the large profits made during the late 1800s, the lumber barons had a great amount of capital available for investing in other industries, particularly flour milling and railroads. The prosperity of the lumber industry also spurred the development of industries related to lumbering, including sash and door factories, linseed oil processors, and manufacturers of tools and fabricated metal parts. The flour industry, in turn, encouraged even more new businesses, like farm implement manufacturers and cooperage firms for making the barrels in which the flour was shipped. As the urban area population continued to increase, more and more products and building materials were needed to service the market, leading to new food industries, foundries, and wool, cotton, and paper mills. And because the flour millers needed a huge supply of money on hand at harvest time to pay farmers,

(Above) A major U.S. city, Minneapolis spans 59 square miles (153 square km). Depending on your plans, you can walk, ride, or drive. Getting around town is a snap. Riding public transportation is a convenient and inexpensive way to get around. Fares range from $1.25 to $2.25, depending on time of day. Additionally, cab services are available anywhere in the metro area. On the horizon, construction is underway in Minneapolis on the long-awaited Light Rail Transit (LRT) system, due to be completed in 2003. LRT is a passenger rail system used in nineteen U.S. metropolitan areas, with a combined average weekday ridership of 800,000. LRT uses trains (called Light Rail Vehicles, or "LRV's") that are smaller than subways ("heavy rail") and intercity passenger trains (like those operated by Amtrak).

(Left) The largest city in Minnesota, Minneapolis is a center of finance, industry, trade, and transportation for the Upper Midwest.

they invested heavily in banks, to gain more control over the money supply. Strengthening the banks helped make the city one of the country's most important financial centers and contributed to Minneapolis' rise as a major insurance center as well. Northwest Bancorporation (now Wells Fargo) and First Bank Stock Corp. (now U.S. Bancorporation),

29

On April 9, 2002, the Greater Minneapolis Convention & Visitors Association (GMCVA) announced the opening of the Minneapolis Convention Center's new expansion project after a three-year renovation process. The expansion project nearly doubled the building's exhibition, meeting, and ballroom space, jumping from 280,000 to 480,000 total square feet. The additional 200,000 square feet of exhibition space and 37 new meeting rooms will allow even larger meetings and conventions to meet in Minneapolis. In fact, more than half of future business secured in 2001 could not have been booked without the expansion of the center.

The St. Paul Companies, Inc. and Northwestern National Life Insurance Company (now ING) can all trace their origins to this period.

Although flour and grain products were still the most valuable products in the Minneapolis economy, the flour-milling industry would fall into a slow decline after 1900, due to increased competition from other U.S. milling centers, the developing Canadian wheat-growing industry, and a reduction in world demand. Unlike the lumber industry, flour millers like General Mills (the successor to the Washburn-Crosby Company) would ultimately survive by diversifying their businesses. Opportunity first presented itself when a hospital dietician accidentally spilled a gruel of wheat bran onto a hot stove. The droplets fried into crisp, tasty flakes that General Mills was quick to realize represented great marketing potential. In 1924, the flakes were introduced as "Wheaties," the first ready-to-eat cereal, and quickly

became the best-selling breakfast food in the country. The die for the future was cast. Seventy-five years later, General Mills and the Pillsbury Company have grown to become prominent suppliers of a multitude of products throughout the supermarket, and have holdings in restaurants and other related industries. Along with Cargill, Inc. and International Multifoods, other turn-of-the-century grain merchants, the companies have grown to become international corporations and major Twin Cities employers.

Other Twin Cities industries would also realize the value of diversification, emphasizing research and development along with sales of their core products. The Twin Cities' best-known example of this strategy is Minnesota Mining and Manufacturing. Founded in 1902 as a sandpaper manufacturer, under the supervision of a young William McKnight the company's innovations would lead to success not just in abrasive materials, but throughout their ever-expanding product lines. Scotch tape, improved audio and video tape, Scotchgard fabric protector, even today's ubiquitous Post-It Notes all had their beginnings in this Twin Cities company, which would eventually abbreviate its name to 3M.

Minneapolis' economic base continued to broaden, fueled by the thousands of new companies that sprang up in the first two decades of the twentieth century. By 1929, printing, publishing, and numerous manufacturing activities were all contributing significantly to the city's economic output. The production of electrical machinery was becoming

an especially important industry, led by the Onan Corporation and Minneapolis Heat Regulator Company (today, Honeywell, Inc.).

During this period, a transportation industry also developed. Along with its extensive railway system, the Twin Cities now had companies in the nascent aviation and airmail industry (including Northwest Airlines), and an automotive assembly plant of the Ford Motor Company. Trucking was becoming big business as well, invaluable to the lucrative wholesaling and retailing trades.

Though St. Paul had the opening advantage in wholesale business due to its heavy steamboat traffic, Minneapolis' steady growth and railroad connections helped close the gap, until it finally exceeded St. Paul in wholesaling volume in 1890. In little more than a decade, Minneapolis would become the state's major retail center as well, with national chains like J.C. Penney; Young Quinlan, the nation's first ready-to-wear women's clothing store; and the establishment of the retailer most identified with Minnesota itself. In 1902, banker and real estate investor George Dayton opened his first department store at 7th and Nicollet, in partnership with the R.S. Goodfellow & Co. chain. Dayton later bought out his partners and renamed the store after himself. Nearly 100

Creation of advanced medical devices is one of Minnesota's premiere industries. Among the world leaders in this business is Medtronic, a developer of cardiac pacemakers and other health products, a *Fortune* 500 company based in Minneapolis.

One of the earliest computers was assembled in Minneapolis in 1946 by Engineering Resource Associates, Inc. (later part of the Sperry Rand Corporation). High technology is still an essential component of the area's economy.

Minneapolis has become the state's retail center, with national chains as well as small, independently owned shops and centers.

years later, the company continues to thrive under its new name, Marshall Fields, and with the addition of its upscale discount chain, Target. First opened in 1962, the chain would eventually become the company's most profitable division.

Agribusiness, manufacturing, finance, and retail would continue to play a large role in Minnesota's economy in the latter half of the twentieth century, but with America's entry into World War II, Minnesota would find a new niche as a center for advanced technology. Companies with government contracts to develop complex defense weaponry and electronic systems would go on to discover commercial applications for the technology in the postwar era, in the manufacturing of drugs, aircraft, electronic components, computers, and lab equipment.

Computers became an especially important industry. In fact, one of the earliest computers was assembled here in 1946 by Engineering Resource Associates, Inc. (later part of the Sperry Rand Corporation). While larger firms like Sperry Rand's Univac Division, Honeywell, and Control Data Corporation maintained the lion's share of the computer manufacturing business, hundreds of smaller firms have found success producing peripheral devices and software, and developing new applications for computing technology.

Many of these skilled electronics and computer technicians went on to combine their knowledge with research from the University of Minnesota and the Mayo Clinic to make the creation of advanced medical devices another of Minnesota's

Target Center opened it doors on October 13, 1990, at the cost of approximately $104,000,000 and took 27 months to complete. The building is situated on one and a half square blocks, encompassing 831,533 square feet. The Target Center main floor is 250' x 88'. It weighs five tons and it can hold 4.1 million pounds. The backstage load-in is 40' x 175' and can hold five semi-trucks unloading at the same time. Target Center has ten floors with 13-foot ceilings and a 2,600-linear-foot catwalk. From the Target Center floor to the top of the ceiling is 101'. The 11,000-square-foot main lobby can accommodate 2,000 people and features one of the largest neon sculptures in the U.S. There are also 15 inside ticket windows for selling and distributing tickets.

premiere industries. Today, several of these local companies rank among world leaders, chief among them Medtronic, a developer of cardiac pacemakers and other health products.

Diversification and innovation. These are the strategies that have taken Minnesota from a vulnerable economy based solely on lumber and flour to one of many profitable industries, broad-based, and thus more resilient. Anchored by powerful corporations in manufacturing, service, and financial industries, and energized by thousands of smaller entrepreneurial companies, Minneapolis is well positioned to maintain its leadership as the American marketplace continues to evolve in response to new technology and societal change. ■

4

CLOUD CITY

*V*enice has its canals, Minneapolis has its skyways—
or so the flattering comparison was made when
the city unveiled its new look in the late 1960s.

It was a renovation eagerly anticipated and long overdue,
driven by economic necessity more than aesthetics and civic
pride. Like most American cities, Minneapolis was rocked by
the prosperity of the post World War II era. As the city
swelled with returning servicemen and businesses created
to handle new demands for consumer goods, housing was
suddenly in short supply. In 1950, Minneapolis' population
reached an all-time high of more that 520,000 people. But
soon after, the population began to drop, as the proliferation
of automobiles and an ever-expanding network of roads and
highways led younger, upwardly mobile couples to
adjacent towns. In first and second-ring suburbs like
Bloomington, Edina, Golden Valley, St. Louis Park, Fridley,
and Roseville, they found ample space for housing. Though
overall population would continue to increase, now the
suburbs, not the central city, would be the beneficiary.

As retailers, factories, warehouses, and offices inevitably
followed the homeowners to the suburbs, Minneapolis stag-
nated. From 1947 to 1958, office space grew at an annual
rate of only one percent per year. Retail sales were lackluster.

(Above) Big enough to boast a postcard-pretty skyline, small enough to
stroll across, downtown Minneapolis offers the best of many different
worlds. You'll find a multitude of restaurants, Broadway theaters, and sports
arenas, not to mention a pedestrian-only boulevard bustling with window
shoppers and people-watchers.

(Left) A unique climate-related addition to the downtown landscape in
more recent years was the development of the skyway system. The first
all-weather pedestrian skyway was built in 1962, spanning 7th Street South
between Marquette and 2nd Avenue. Today more than fifty blocks are con-
nected by these second story walkways. In addition to providing all-season
convenience for downtown residents, employees, and visitors, the skyway
system connects numerous and varied retail outlets. It is reported that
downtown Minneapolis has more retail outlets in a four-block area than any
other city in the country.

Large tracts of land stood abandoned by migrating businesses
and much of downtown's remaining buildings were in deteri-
orating condition, while traffic congestion and parking
problems increased. Blighted blocks, empty store fronts,
and darkened theatre marquees had robbed downtown
Minneapolis of the vitality and importance it had enjoyed
since the city's earliest days.

Abundant planting, seating, fountains, and public art enrich the central urban setting of downtown.

It was at this point that a model for the future appeared, and it was not one welcomed by the struggling downtown businesses. In 1956, Southdale, the first enclosed shopping mall in the United States, opened in Edina. With dozens of shops all under one roof, joined by a year-round garden court with art and seating, the concept proved irresistible to shoppers, particularly during Minnesota's long, severe winters. More "Dales" followed in other Twin Cities suburbs, until the downtowns of both Minneapolis and St. Paul were surrounded by competing shopping malls of spacious modern buildings, popular retailers, and a sea of free parking.

Fearing for its survival, Minneapolis' downtown business community formed the Downtown Council, and with the City Planning Commission set about revitalizing the central business district. Key to their plans was the renovation of Nicollet Avenue, the downtown's primary retail corridor.

In 1966, eight blocks of the street were closed to cars and trucks and an expansive open-air pedestrian mall was constructed, with landscaping, fountains, and a narrow winding roadway for public transportation. Upon its completion a year later, foot traffic and retail sales improved dramatically. The downtown area regained both significant market share and its image as the heart of the city.

Simultaneously, a system of second-story skyways was slowly constructed to connect major downtown buildings. Designed as a modern, convenient way to move shoppers between stores, office buildings, and parking ramps, these glass-enclosed walkways have come to be closely associated with the city of Minneapolis. Like the suburban malls, skyways give shoppers access to a variety of stores without having to deal with the worst extremes of Minnesota weather. Now having grown to more than forty skyways, the system wanders more than five miles through the downtown area, and has created a second retail corridor above the streets. This bustling thoroughfare is lined with

specialty shops, convenience stores, and restaurants, as well as services such as dry cleaners, hair stylists, florists, photo developers, and financial services.

A third milestone in Minneapolis' renewal was the completion of the IDS Center in 1973. Designed by architect Phillip Johnson, the 57-story skyscraper dominated the skyline and was hailed around the world for its elegant simplicity. With its central location on Nicollet Mall between Seventh and Eighth streets, and skyways converging on it from all four directions, the IDS Center and its nine-story, glass-roofed courtyard has become a kind of town square for the city.

Its retail base strengthened, Minneapolis turned next to the historic preservation of its oldest buildings. Careful restorations created attractive space for offices, restaurants and arts organizations in venerable buildings like Butler Square, the Lumber Exchange Building, and the old Masonic Temple (now the Hennepin Center For The Arts). The Foshay Tower, patterned after the Washington Monument

Located on the west side of the Marquette Plaza office building is the 1.5-acre Cancer Survivors Park plaza. In partnership with the City of Minneapolis, the area represents the only public park in downtown Minneapolis. Situated at the north end of Nicollet Mall, the park offers a gathering place downtown featuring a central fountain and numerous seating areas amidst lush green landscaping.

and for forty years the tallest building of the city, found new appreciation for its stately appearance and stands defiantly in the shadow of the IDS Center. Though much of old Minneapolis near the St. Anthony Falls was leveled during the sweeping Gateway project of the late 1960s, the remaining area was designated a historic district, as were several blocks of former warehouses on the downtown's western border.

But the most explosive growth would come in the 1980s. One hundred years after the city's first construction boom, once again, new buildings were filling out the skyline at a

The block formerly known as "E" is taking shape as an exciting new entertainment complex, virtually guaranteed to bring new life to its stretch of
Hennepin Avenue. Opened in August 2002, the new hot spot offers
entertainment options to folks of all ages. Among the new establishments
housed there are Chart House, Gordon Biersch Brewing Company, Hard
Rock Café, and GameWorks. Pictured is "Block E" under construction in
early 2002; see page 8, the Chamber Foreword, for a more recent shot of
Block E just before its completion, in late August 2002.

breathtaking pace. Nearly $4 billion was spent on office
construction during the decade, most notably on Norwest
Center (now Wells Fargo Center), whose stylish art deco
façade was designed by Cesar Pelli, and the Piper Jaffrey
Tower with its intriguing asymmetrical profiles. Today, more
than 123,000 people now work in downtown offices and
stores. And renewed interest in urban living has led to a
rise in demand for downtown residential space.

The city has also continued to bolster its appeal to
shoppers. Dayton's (now Marshall Fields), the city's oldest
and best-known department store, has been joined by the
addition of new upscale developments, most notably Gaviidae
Commons, home of Saks Fifth Avenue and Nieman Marcus.
Even the Nicollet Mall, still vibrant but showing its age after
twenty years, received a facelift in 1990.

One block to the west, Hennepin Avenue has shown new
signs of life as well. The worst of the buildings—and the
undesirable businesses they housed—were removed and a

concerted effort was undertaken to return the street to its
roots as the city's premiere entertainment district. The
Orpheum and State theatres, structures dating back to the
1920s, were refurbished for touring Broadway shows and
concerts. Other smaller theatres opened, along with restaurants
catering to theatergoers. And after years of development,
Hennepin Avenues "Block E" entertainment complex is
finally completed, an enclosed block-square mix
of movie theatres, retail space, night clubs, and a hotel.

Another block over, the glitz of Hennepin Avenue segues
into the brick and neon of the Warehouse District, currently
one of the most trendy and lively sections of downtown.
Within these renovated buildings, more than thirty bars,
restaurants, music clubs, and art galleries each week draw
thousands of young people, not just from throughout the
city, but from the suburbs as well.

Thanks to a proactive business community and innovative
concepts in building and design, Minneapolis' downtown area
has not only survived the threat of suburban competition, it's
prospered. Like the skyways that connect its buildings, the
interconnected relationship of its stores, offices, entertainment
venues, and residential spaces is the key to Minneapolis'
continued vitality. ■

Star of the North

From the outside the Lumber Exchange Building does appear mammoth and rough-hewn. However, from the inside, because of care taken when remodeling or because of the current clientele, a mixture of graphic and other artists and law firms, there is much to admire. The Lumber Exchange was designed in 1885 by architects Franklin B. Long (1842-1912) and Frederick Kees (1852-1927). The design is called Richardsonian Romanesque, a design also found in the Hennepin County Courthouse and Hennepin Center for the Arts. The Lumber Exchange was the first skyscraper in Minneapolis and one of the first fireproof buildings in the country.

A common tenant of downtown revitalization efforts is the preservation and restoration of historic buildings. Rather than demolishing these denizens of history, communities are working to transform them into thriving office buildings, residences and commerce centers.

5

NEIGHBORS

erhaps one of the most surprising aspects of the Twin Cities is Minneapolis' and St. Paul's continued existence as separate cities. It's a credit to each city that they have both managed to integrate their economic and social lives so thoroughly, yet still retain their own identities.

Minneapolis takes pride in its status as a modern American city, ever changing, ever exciting, and alive with the hustle-bustle of daily life. St. Paul, on the other hand, with its Victorian charms and quieter downtown, is considered by its residents as a kind of sanctuary from its "big city" sister, more friendly, more stable, and more conducive to family life.

Of course, like any siblings, rivalry is common, and for Minneapolis and St. Paul, goes back to their earliest days. Competition was intense as each city vied for recognition as the Upper Midwest's premiere city. Local newspapers not only joined in, but often heated up the battle. The census of 1890, which showed Minneapolis had at last surpassed its rival in population, was especially stinging to St. Paul's collective ego. Nevertheless, the generations-long feud has continued to the present day, although the intensity has mellowed to a more good-natured ribbing among old friends. Occasionally, though, the competitive spirit can resurface as strong as ever, such as when the location of a corporate headquarters or major league sports team is at stake.

(Above) Minneapolis' closest neighbor and sister city is Saint Paul, the state capitol. People in the area feel so much a part of a regional community that they often say they live in "Minneapolis-Saint Paul."

(Left) According to capitol historians, the statue on top of the Minnesota Capitol is a Daniel Chester French sculpture titled "Progress of the State." The horses stand for Earth, Wind, Fire, Water—the four elements of the physical world as taught in classical Greek studies. The two women who stand beside the horses symbolize Industry and Agriculture. Together they are Civilization. The man who sits high on top is Prosperity. All constituents represent progression and thus the statues name, "Progress of the State."

Despite these emotional divisions, the physical boundaries between the cities—except where formed by the Mississippi River—are indistinguishable. In daily life, residents cross between the cities for business, shopping, and socializing with no more notice than they'd give to crossing a street.

St. Paul can be confusing to non-residents due to street names that are neither numbered nor alphabetized, but it has sights that more than make up for the inconvenience. Travel Summit Avenue, a wide, elm-lined street that cuts east to west across the city, and you'll see miles of Victorian mansions, churches, the governor's residence, and two colleges. As it nears downtown St. Paul, Summit Avenue passes by the Cathedral of St. Paul, one of the largest church buildings in

The Minnesota World Trade Center, visible here through the windows of the City Center shopping mall in Saint Paul, was built with forty stories in 1987 and became the first international trade center in the Midwest.

North America. Construction began in 1904 and took nearly fifty years to complete the 300-foot-high, domed church that overlooks the downtown area.

The Cathedral is bookended across Interstate 94 and a large grassy mall by the State Capitol. Designed by St. Paul architect Cass Gilbert in 1895, the Capitol's Italian-Renaissance dome is adorned by gleaming statues of a golden charioteer and his team of golden horses. Gilbert won national acclaim for his design, which was modeled after St. Peter's Church in Rome. One of downtown's other most striking buildings is Landmark Center, a castle-like structure with turrets around the roofline and two towers. It opened in 1902 as the Federal Courts Building, but when the government finally outgrew the space, the city saved it from the wrecking ball and renovated it into a home for arts, historical, and educational organizations.

St. Paul, like Minneapolis, is serviced by several freeways, providing easy access between the cities and all the surrounding suburbs. Add to that ample public transportation, and the amenities of the entire metropolitan area are within easy reach to all. Surely the best-known shopping mall, not just in the Twin Cities, but the entire world, is Mall of America in the nearby suburb of Bloomington. Skeptics were vocal during its construction, but since its opening in 1992, few Twin Citians have been able to resist its allure of 500 stores and eateries and Knott's Camp Snoopy indoor amusement park. Of course, nearly every suburb boasts some form of shopping mall or retail area and none tonier than those in Edina, the southwestern suburb with the upscale Southdale and Galleria malls, and the boutiques at 50th and France Avenues that cater to their well-off residents.

The neighboring city of Shakopee, just across the Mississippi River Valley south of Minneapolis, has attractions for people of all ages. Valleyfair Amusement Park has seventy-five rides and shows, including five rollercoasters. Canterbury Park Racetrack features thoroughbred racing and Raceway Park has NASCAR competitions. Mystic Lake Casino has more than three thousand slot machines, plus blackjack, poker, and big-name entertainment. And the annual

The impressive Mall of America is located in the southern suburb of Bloomington, just minutes from downtown Minneapolis. The nation's largest shopping and entertainment complex is visited by more than 40 million people a year, and is anchored by Macy's, Nordstrom, Bloomingdale's, and Sears. In addition to the 500-plus stores, exciting attractions keep visitors busy for hours. Visitors can bowl, play video games, shoot a game of putt-putt golf, see a movie, hear a stand-up comedy routine, and ride a roller coaster without stepping foot outside.

For those always on the lookout for a great deal, the Twin Cities area offers several outlet malls with discounted merchandise. At the Medford Outlet Center, fifty miles south of Minneapolis, shoppers will find Nike, Liz Claiborne, Mikasa and Columbia Sportswear at great values. Trek to the Tanger Outlet Center, forty miles north of the Twin Cities, for steals on Reebok, Levi's, Nine West, Bugle Boy and more. For a short drive and big savings, try the Horizon Outlet Center in Woodbury. Pick up your favorites in Eddie Bauer, Casual Corner, Hush Puppies, Jones New York, and more.

The Minneapolis Aquatennial is an annual celebration that draws people from throughout the region. Activities include an AirExpo, sailing, tennis, bowling, music, Hennepin Avenue Block Party, parades, park events, canoe races, arts and crafts fairs, a sand-castle building competition, volleyball, fireworks, and the famous Milk Carton Boat Races.

Renaissance Festival will transport you back to a 16th century medieval village for a day of revelry.

St. Paul's Como Zoo is a popular destination for families, along its turn-of-the-century carousel and the botanical wonders of its Conservatory. But an even larger zoo is located just south of the city in Apple Valley. At the Minnesota Zoo, indoor and outdoor walking trails take you past animals in natural and recreated habitats. Another fun day trip, less than thirty minutes from downtown St. Paul, is the historic town of Stillwater, on the St. Croix River. Once a center of commerce for fur traders, trappers, and lumbermen, the town now attracts antique hunters, antiquarian book collectors, and sightseers. ■

Canterbury Park Racetrack and Card Club is the number-one year-round
destination for the intelligent player. Located in Shakopee, Minnesota,
Canterbury Park is just twenty-five minutes from both downtown
Minneapolis and St. Paul. Canterbury's one-mile oval is one of the finest
in the nation. It features sandy loam composition and three chutes—
3 1/2 furlongs, 6 1/2 furlongs, and 1 1/4 miles. The turf course is a 7/8
mile inner oval that accommodates races at several distances.

Mystic Lake Casino is located just
minutes from the Twin Cities of
Minneapolis and Saint Paul. It offers
high-stakes bingo in its 1,000 seat
bingo hall and more than 2,500 slot
machines, as well as more than 140
blackjack tables in its beautiful casino.
It also provides an elegant 325-seat
buffet style restaurant featuring
four-star cuisine, as well as an award-
winning steakhouse and 24-hour cafe.
It is located only 25 minutes from
Mall of America.

The Valleyfair Amusement Park is a 100-acre park opened in 1976, and features the most thrilling and unusual rides in the area. Each year new attractions are added to the mix, such as the Wild Thing, a 207-foot tall roller coaster that reaches speeds of 78 miles per hour, and a 180-foot free fall. The park also has an IMAX theater, a waterpark, multiple children's areas, live music, shows, and other attractions. The season usually runs from early May to October.

History comes alive at many of Minnesota's historic sites that offer visitors an opportunity to see what life was like in earlier days. Young and old alike enjoy hands-on activities that teach about early settlers, forts and military history, Victorian customs and traditions, fur trading and exploring, and many other aspects of the area's past.

"The Mall of America has had a tremendous impact on the image and marketing of the city of Bloomington as a destination. It's part of a package for visitors. Many out of town visitors come here for a Twins game or a basketball game, and take a side trip to the mall. There is a very significant financial impact in the city and the region. The biggest impact is in our hospitality industry, which is our number one industry—our hotels, motels, and restaurants, and that also supports our convention industry. Business leaders agree the mall is very beneficial to the Twin Cities area and the state of Minnesota."

Clark Arneson
Manager of Planning & Development
City of Bloomington

Minnesota's excellent zoo has more than twenty-seven hundred animals living in their "natural" habitats. A highlight is the new Discovery Bay aquarium center, a $25 million maze of underground tunnels and walkways that bring you face-to-face with sharks and rays. There's also a tidal pool and dolphin tank. The Minnesota Trail presents fifty-nine species indigenous to Minnesota, such as lynx, pumas, and beavers. The Northern Trail recreates the harsh winter conditions of North America, from tundra to taiga (mixed evergreen forests).

6

ARTS AT HEART

s far back as the late 1880s, Minneapolitans embraced fine arts and the theatre. But it took the opening of the Guthrie Theatre in 1963 to convince the rest of the country.

Sir Tyrone Guthrie was a visionary director from Ireland who dreamed of expanding serious theatre into America's heartland. After touring several cities, he chose Minneapolis as the home for his theatre company, recognizing the city's widespread support of the arts. The perceptiveness of his choice was affirmed when an army of volunteers raised the $2 million needed to begin construction on the building and its unique octagonal thrust stage. The first season included performances of Shakespeare's *Hamlet*, Chekhov's *Three Sisters*, and Miller's *Death Of A Salesman*. In the nearly thirty years since, the Guthrie has won international acclaim for its productions of classical, contemporary, and experimental drama. Its thirty-one thousand season-ticket holders exceeds that of any other theatre in the country.

Additionally, Twin Citians support some thirty other legitimate theatre companies, many of them also nationally known, including the Actors Theatre, Theatre In The Round, the Children's Theatre Company, Theatre de la Jeune Lune, Mixed Blood, and Penumbra. Broadway touring companies are regularly showcased in Hennepin Avenues historic State

(Above) The Twin Cities boast more theater seats per capita than any other U.S. metropolitan area outside of New York City. With more than thirty small theater venues sprinkled throughout the city, Minneapolis is home to a strong theater scene filled with ballets, cabarets, comedies and other unique performances. In addition, large Broadway productions, such as "Victor Victoria" and Disney's "The Lion King," often debut at the Historic State and Orpheum theatres, located in the bustling Hennepin Avenue Theatre District in downtown Minneapolis. The city's regional theater jewel, the Guthrie Theater (pictured), consistently presents critically acclaimed contemporary and classic performances.

(Left) The Sculpture Garden, adjacent to the Walker Art Center, is another of the Twin Cities' renowned sights, with imaginative contemporary works spread across leafy parkland. The blockbuster piece is Claes Oldenburg's and Coosje van Bruggen's *Spoonbridge and Cherry*, a sculpture-fountain combo built around a 52-foot spoon cradling a massive red cherry.

and Orpheum Theatres. The nation's largest professional dinner theatre can be found in the southwestern suburb of Chanhassen. Live performances of Garrison Keillor's popular radio program, "A Prairie Home Companion," are featured at St. Paul's Fitzgerald Theatre. And the Brave New Workshop, founded in 1958, is now the longest running satirical comedy theatre in the United States.

Orchestra Hall, home of the internationally acclaimed Minnesota Orchestra, features a minimalist auditorium that seats 2,400, and has a large main floor with three balconies symmetrically girding it. Behind the natural wooden stage and on the ceiling loom what look like enormous sugar cubes hurled by some mythical giant. These blocks provide hundreds of surfaces that deflect sound, making Orchestra Hall among the most acoustically perfect theaters in the nation. You can hear from anywhere in the house.

Another prominent figure in Minneapolis' cultural history is lumber baron Thomas Barlow Walker. One of the nation's ten wealthiest men by 1923, Walker first displayed his art collection in a building constructed near his home. It was the first art gallery in the area and as Walker's collection expanded, so did the building, until the gallery was moved to its present site in 1927. Known today as the Walker Art Center, the institution has grown into one of the nation's finest museums for modern art and performances of music and dance, experimental theatre, and avant-garde movies. Its permanent collection has examples of European modernism, cubism, abstract expressionism, and minimalism. Exhibits have included the works of Willem de Kooning, Alexander Calder, Henri Matisse, and Pablo Picasso.

The Twin Cities other major art museum, the Minneapolis Institute of Arts, can also trace its origins back

Known globally as a leader in teaching, research, and public service, the University of Minnesota, Twin Cities, consistently ranks among the top 20 public universities in the nation. The classic Big 10 campus, located in the heart of the Minneapolis-St. Paul metropolitan area, provides a world-class setting for lifelong learning. More than 150 bachelor's degrees, 200 master's degrees, and 100 doctoral degrees make the University of Minnesota, Twin Cities, one of the most comprehensive institutions in the country. The University community is a broad mix of ethnic backgrounds, interests, and cultures. Students come from all 50 states and more than 100 foreign countries. The University of Minnesota, Twin Cities, is also a thriving center for culture and the arts, featuring outstanding galleries, museums, concerts, theater productions, and public lectures. For sports fans, the Golden Gophers offer all the spirit and excitement of Division I college athletics.

The University of St. Thomas, founded in 1885 by Archbishop John Ireland, is a Catholic, independent, liberal arts, archdiocesan university that emphasizes values-centered, career-oriented education. With a record-high 11,570 students (fall 2001), St. Thomas is Minnesota's largest independent college or university. St. Thomas has been coeducational at the undergraduate level since 1977 and welcomes students of all ages and nationalities and from all religious, racial, ethnic, and financial backgrounds.

"I chose to attend Augsburg because of my family's ties to the college and its location in the city. What makes me most proud of Augsburg, however, is the great job they do in seeking out students who reflect the growing diversity in our community. Augsburg steps out beyond what is traditional and comfortable with the intent and determination to meet the challenge of educating students with different learning needs, physical requirements, and cultural backgrounds."

Senator Julie Sabo
Minnesota State Senate
Augsburg College Alumna

Augsburg College is located in the heart of the Twin Cities of Minneapolis and St. Paul with a growing program in Rochester. As the Evangelical Lutheran Church in America's (ELCA) most diverse and only urban institution, Augsburg strives to educate both traditional and non-traditional students, offering undergraduate degrees in more than fifty major areas of study. The College also grants four graduate degrees: the Master of Arts in Leadership, the Master of Social Work, the Master of Arts in Nursing, and the Master of Science in Physician Assistant Studies, the state's only Physician Assistant training program.

8

MAJOR LEAGUE CITY

"A cold Omaha."

That was how former Minnesota Senator Hubert Humphrey once described what Minneapolis would be like without professional major league sports. Looking past the hyperbole, the statement well reflects the attitudes—and fears—of a great many local sports fans and civic boosters. The Twin Cities has long looked upon the presence of professional sports teams as not just a source of entertainment but as recognition of their status as a major metropolitan area. Major league baseball, football, basketball, and hockey teams are viewed as being as integral to the area's quality of life as the park system and cultural opportunities.

Except for the Duluth Eskimos pro football team in the 1920s, Minnesota sports in the first half of the 20th century were strictly a minor league affair. Baseball was especially popular, going back all the way to 1884. In what was probably the most good-natured expression of the reoccurring rivalry between Minneapolis and St. Paul, each city had its own team. The Minneapolis Millers played first in a small downtown stadium one block west of Hennepin Avenue (today, the site of Butler Square), then moved to a ballpark in South Minneapolis. The Saint Paul Saints also had their own downtown field for a time, but played mainly in the Midway area. It became a tradition for the archrivals to play each other in a doubleheader, one game in each ballpark, on the summer holidays of Memorial Day, Independence Day, and Labor Day.

(Above) Minnesota baseball fans love to cheer on the Twins. Pictured is 2001 Gold Glove winning centerfielder Torii Hunter. Photo courtesy Minnesota Twins.

(Left) Kevin Garnett, number 21 of the Minnesota Timberwolves, dunks against the Cleveland Cavaliers during the NBA game at the Target Center in Minneapolis during the 2001-02 season. Photo by David Sherman/NBAE/Getty Images

By the 1950s, however, minor league teams weren't enough, and both cities stepped up their efforts to attract a major league team, sometimes working together, other times in competition with each other. Each city went even so far as to build its own stadium. Finally, late in 1960, Calvin Griffith, president of the American League's Washington Senators, agreed to move his team to the state and the Twin Cities had a major league ball club for the following season. Renamed the Minnesota Twins, the team played in Bloomington's Metropolitan Stadium (now the site of Mall of America) for the next twenty years, winning the American League pennant in 1965 and fielding the legendary home-run hitter Harmon Killebrew.

The completion of the Hubert H. Humphrey Metrodome in 1981 brought professional baseball to downtown Minneapolis, in an unusual indoor stadium whose domed roof was formed of layers of woven fiberglass material held

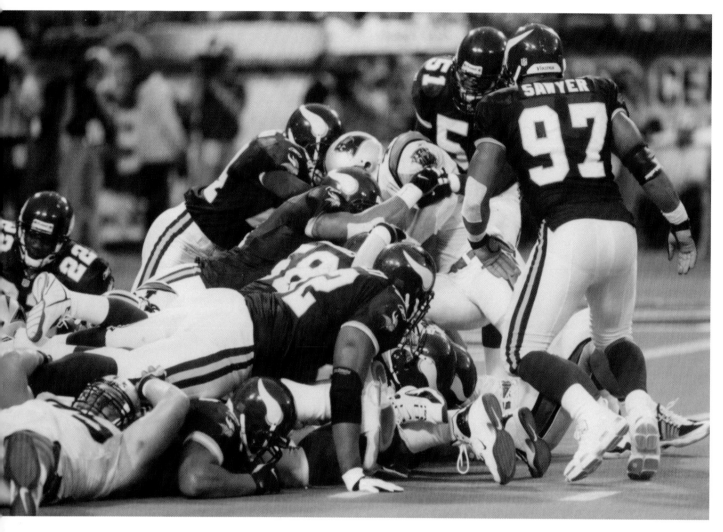

Fans pack the Metrodome every fall as the Minnesota Vikings take the field for National Football League (NFL) action. Pictured, the Viking defense puts up a wall on their opponent during the 2001 season. Photo by Rick Kolodziej, Minnesota Vikings

aloft by powerful electric fans. More than one observer has noted the building's similarity that of a soufflé or an over-padded ottoman. However ambivalent fans became about the Metrodome, especially as outdoor ballparks became popular again in the 1990s, it will always have the distinction of being the home of the Twins during their two World Series victories, in 1982 and 1991.

Along with the Twins, 1961 was also the inaugural year of the Minnesota Vikings, the National Football League's newest expansion team. Led by Hall of Fame quarterback Fran Tarkenton, the team took to the field in Metropolitan Stadium, and fans still remember, with awe and nostalgia, games played in freezing temperatures, rain, mud, sleet, and early winter snow. The Vikings followed the Twins to the Metrodome in 1981. The Vikings have made three Super Bowl appearances and are easily Minnesota's most popular team. "Purple Pride" (named for the team color) seems on display everywhere in the city each year during football season.

Basketball was Minnesota's first modern big-league sport, beginning with the Minnesota Lakers in 1947. The team enjoyed several years of national and world championships, but as the team's aging stars retired, Minneapolis' interest waned. When the franchise moved to Los Angeles in 1960, it would be thirty years before the National Basketball League returned to the city. Ultimately, it took the persistence of two local businessmen and a former Laker, George Mikan, to convince the NBA to add a Minneapolis franchise for the 1989 season. The Minnesota Timberwolves set attendance records in their first season and have remained a hot ticket ever since. After several disappointing seasons, the team hit its stride under head coach Flip Saunders and star forward Kevin Garnett, breaking previous records for games won per season and advancing to the playoffs for three consecutive seasons.

Hockey, of course, would seem a natural fit for Minnesota, and in 1967 the state landed its first National Hockey League franchise by promising to build a big-league arena (the lack of adequate facilities had helped drive the Lakers out of town). Metropolitan Sports Center, constructed adjacent to Metropolitan Stadium, remained the home of the Minnesota North Stars through twenty-six years and through two Stanley Cup finals, until the team moved to Dallas in 1993.

Neither rain nor snow prevents sports-mad fans from worshipping at
their domed downtown temple, the 62,000-seat Hubert H. Humphrey
Metrodome. It's home to the Vikings (professional football), Twins
(professional baseball), and Gophers (college football).

The new RiverCentre (Xcel Energy Center) is the home of the Minnesota Wild NHL hockey team, one of the area's newest major-league attractions. The RiverCentre is a multipurpose arena, auditorium, trade show, and meeting space, and is the site for many conventions and sporting events like the State High School hockey and basketball championships.

Almost immediately, talk began of luring the NHL back to Minnesota. Attempts to bring the Edmonton Oilers, the Winnipeg Jets, and the Hartford Whalers all failed. St. Paul's mayor, Norm Coleman, proved instrumental in the fight, winning support for a state-of-the-art arena in downtown St. Paul that was key to winning another franchise in 1997. After three years of growing anticipation, the Minnesota Wild took to the ice in the Xcel Energy Center in September 2000, and even supporters seemed surprised by the crowds, which quickly dispelled any lingering doubts about the Twin Cities' commitment to professional hockey.

Beyond the "big four" of professional sports, Minnesota also has its own professional soccer team, The Minnesota Thunder, at the National Sports Center just north of Minneapolis. The Minnesota Lynx, part of the Women's National Basketball League, plays in Target Center. And three decades after the Millers and the Saints left town, a re-formed St. Paul Saints is again playing minor league ball in St. Paul's

Midway Stadium. The blend of outdoor baseball, a small-town atmosphere (a freight train occasionally chugs by just beyond the outfield wall), and between-innings shenanigans regularly attracts sell-out crowds. The live pig mascot that delivers the balls to the pitcher is probably better known than any of the players on the team. ■

The Minnesota Wild sparked an instant fan base when they came to the Twin Cities in 2000. Photo by Bruce Kluckhohn Photography, courtesy Minnesota Wild.

9

CITY ON THE MOVE

t's purely coincidental that the roller skate was gaining in popularity about the same time the Minneapolis park system was conceived, but from the vantage point of today, they would indeed seem made for each other.

Even as Minneapolis's urban area took shape during the building boom of the 1880s, civic leaders were also determined to balance the development with the need for public spaces. To this end, the Minneapolis Park Board was created in 1883 and charged with planning a system of parks to beautify the city, enhance the urban quality of life, and provide recreational opportunities accessible to the entire population.

The Park Board enlisted the help of Horace W. S. Cleveland, a well-known Chicago landscape architect who had previously worked with St. Paul on the formation of their own park system. Cleveland had a passion for intelligent long-range planning and was inspired by the example of New York's Central Park. For Minneapolis, he outlined a system of parks and scenic boulevards that meandered through the city. The plan was attacked by some as a needless extravagance, but Cleveland insisted that

Aptly named the City of Lakes, Minneapolis is home to more than twenty within the city limits alone. The number increases dramatically as you move out into the suburbs. And don't let our "Land of 10,000 Lakes" motto fool you—there are actually well over 15,000 lakes in our beautiful state.

Minneapolis land values would increase and that, in turn, would increase property tax revenues for the city. Ultimately, the plan was approved, parks were created and landscaped, swamps were drained, and lakeshores firmed up to create the Chain Of Lakes park system that has become one of Minneapolis' proudest achievements.

The Chain of Lakes connects the five lakes in South Minneapolis—Brownie Lake, Cedar Lake, Lake of the Isles, Lake Calhoun, and Lake Harriet—with paved pedestrian and biking paths. On sunny summer days, it can seem like most of the city is out walking, jogging, swimming, biking, in-line skating, or just sitting in the shade of lakeside trees. On the lakes themselves, you'll see people sailboarding, windsurfing, canoeing, and fishing.

With lakes such a big part of the geography and culture, perhaps it was inevitable that Minneapolis would create a summer celebration around them, and beginning in 1940,

67

Outdoor enthusiasts enjoy water sports throughout the year, with options including swimming, fishing (including ice fishing), skiing, skating, boating, and more.

that's exactly what happened. Today, the Minneapolis Aquatennial is an annual ten-day event in late July. Some 800,000 people each year join in more than 250 festivities that make the most of the city's parks and lakes. Perhaps the most unusual event is the Milk Carton Boat Race, in which entrants compete with self-designed, quirky vessels made of empty milk cartons. Initiated in 1971 as a promotion for a milk distributor, the outrageous race has become one of the

Aquatennial's most popular attractions. Of course, more traditional boat and sailing races are held as well, along with sand-castle sculpting contests, the Queen of the Lakes pageant, parades, and a huge fireworks show along the downtown riverfront.

Meanwhile, across the river and half a year away, St. Paul has its own celebration—one that's the perfect counterpart to the Aquatennial. The St. Paul Winter Carnival, which holds the dubious distinction of being the oldest cold weather festival in America, was founded in 1886 for the purpose of showing the world that Minnesota winters were snowy and cold, yes, but could actually be fun as well. Such a celebration was

inconceivable to Minneapolis civic leaders, who, as a policy, maintained their winters were actually quite mild (despite the fact that the 1880s saw three straight winters with mean temperatures in the single digits). St. Paul, however, enthusiastically embraced both the reality of the climate and the idea of a winter festival with an ice palace as its signature. More than a hundred years later, the Winter Carnival has grown into an annual celebration that includes a treasure hunt, snowmobile race, ice sculptures, ski-jumping and ice-fishing contests, and a full-blown mythology concerning warring kingdoms of ice and fire. The 1992 ice palace rose to 150 feet, setting a record for the world's largest ice structure.

But celebrations in the Twin Cities aren't limited to these two extremes. If anything, people here seem to exhibit endless creativity in filling the calendar with celebrations, community festivals, and all manner of noteworthy special events. St. Patrick's Day, as you might expect, is a major event in St. Paul, with its prominent Irish heritage. A boisterous parade kicks off the revelry, which then moves into the dozens of Irish pubs that dot the city. Not to be outdone, the Swedish population gathers in Minneapolis' Minnehaha Park in late June for Svenskarnes Dag, or Swedes Day, with Scandinavian food, music, and dancing. Other ethnic cultures in the Twin Cities hold their own events, too, and virtually every group comes together in April to share folk art and cultural entertainment at the Festival Of Nations.

At its birth in the mid 1800s the Minneapolis Farmers Market was the primary place for small Minneapolis corner grocers to purchase fresh produce and locally produced farmstead products at fair prices. In the 1970s, consumers began to bypass these grocers in favor of purchasing directly from the Farmers Market. The Minneapolis Farmers Market began to flourish into a retail market and eventually evolved into today's successful marketplace. The Nicollet Mall Farmers Market is an extension of the main market. Located on the sidewalks of the Nicollet Mall in downtown Minneapolis, between 5th and 10th Streets, the Minneapolis Farmers Market calls this spot home every week on Thursdays and Saturdays.

People of all ages enjoy participating in competitive and recreational sporting events throughout the Minneapolis-St. Paul area, and there is a wide variety of activities from which to choose. In addition to being good for the body, many events also are good for the soul, providing an opportunity for promoting worthwhile causes and raising money for charitable organizations throughout the area.

Golf could be called the most popular recreational activity in the Twin Cities, which boasts more golfers per capita than any other city in the nation and more than 100 golf courses, both public and private. Minnesota has hosted several prestigious golf tournaments, including the 1991 U.S. Open at Hazeltine National Golf Club in Chaska, and the 2002 PGA Championship in August 2002.

The Fourth of July Weekend is highlighted by the Taste of Minnesota Festival, held on the lawn of the State Capitol. More than forty local restaurants tempt you with their specialties, while several stages present a wide range of music, capped by a sensational fireworks show at dusk. Classical music is the focus of the Minnesota Orchestra Summer Music Festival, on Peavey Plaza outside Orchestra Hall in midsummer. Street fairs and art shows fill the weekends from spring through fall, including the Uptown Art Fair in south Minneapolis and St. Paul's Grand Old Day. Of particular note is the Stone Arch Festival of the Arts, at the historic stone arch bridge across the Falls of St. Anthony. Built by the Great Northern Railway in 1883 and still one of Minnesota's greatest works of architecture, the bridge was converted to a pedestrian walkway in the mid 1990s.

The summer celebrations climax with the Minnesota State Fair, an annual event in the state dating back to 1859. The establishment of a permanent fairgrounds was yet another source of heated rivalry between the cities in the late nineteenth

The holiday season is its own special event, as the city gets decked out in
her seasonal splendor of twinkling lights and brightly colored banners, and
shoppers crowd the stores in search of the perfect stocking stuffer.

The Uptown Art Fair began thirty-nine years ago as a neighborhood art sale just down the block from what is now Calhoun Square in Minneapolis. Today, artists, tourists, art lovers, and festival goers from around the country enjoy Minnesota's annual outdoor event.

century, but ultimately St. Paul prevailed with the 210-acre site that the fair still occupies today. Over the decades, it has grown into one of the largest state fairs in the country, preserving its agricultural focus but adding attractions to appeal to the metropolitan fairgoers as well.

No December holiday season is complete without taking in the Holidazzle Parade on Nicollet Mall. Floats are lit up like Christmas trees and even the people dressed as story-book characters are covered in countless tiny lights. Based on the popular "electric parades" of Walt Disney World, the Holidazzle Parade draws thousands of shoppers and families to downtown Minneapolis. The year ends with the Capitol City New Year celebration, featuring a New Year's Eve count-down in downtown St. Paul that is patterned after the one in New York's Times Square.

All things considered, it probably takes more effort to be bored in the Twin Cities than just about anywhere. ■

In 1883, the Minneapolis Park and Recreation Board (MPRB) was created by an act of the Minnesota Legislature to serve as an independently elected, semi-autonomous body responsible for maintaining and developing the Minneapolis Park system to meet the needs of citizens of Minneapolis. Recreational, environmental, and other park programs and services are provided for all ages and abilities, from toddlers to senior citizens. The Minneapolis Park System consists of more than 170 park properties, including local and regional parks, playgrounds, tot lots, triangles, golf courses, gardens, picnic areas, biking and walking paths, nature sanctuaries, and a 55-mile parkway system. Together, these properties total nearly 6,400 acres of land and water.

10

QUALITY AND SPIRIT

homas B. Walker originated the Minneapolis Institute of Arts. James J. Hill was the chief patron of the St. Paul Public Library. John Pillsbury made the University of Minnesota his personal cause.

The lumber, milling, and railroad magnates who built the Minneapolis economy also established a tradition of altruism that has been continued to this day by Twin Cities companies. Undoubtedly, there is an element of public relations behind much corporate giving, and a certain amount of self-interest as well. Owners of the many large companies headquartered in Minneapolis and St. Paul benefit from the high quality of life in the areas in which they and their employees live. But above such concerns is a more simple motivation. Companies return wealth in the form of donations and grants because in the Twin Cities business community, it is recognized as the right thing to do.

One of the most notable examples of this is the Minnesota Keystone Program. Its origins go back to 1946, when the Dayton's department store became the second company in the nation to commit five percent of its pre-tax profits to

In addition to performing the more well-known work of helping under-privileged families acquire and build a home of their own, Twin Cities Habitat for Humanity's Mortgage Foreclosure Prevention Program (MFPP) was established in July 1993. Keeping families in their homes is a perfect adjunct to Habitat's traditional homeownership program. MFPP was taken from a concept originated at Northside Residents Redevelopment Council (NRRC) in Minneapolis, and developed with funding from the Family Housing Fund and Northwest Area Foundation. The program was piloted in St. Paul, Minnesota; Iowa, Idaho, and Oregon. As part of this pilot project the Twin Cities MFPP serviced an area in South Minneapolis in which foreclosures were rising dramatically. In addition to families losing their homes, the possibility of homes lying vacant and being vandalized after foreclosure negatively impacted the larger community. In 1994 both Habitat and NRRC expanded their service areas to serve all homeowners in Minneapolis, NRRC serving North and Northeast Minneapolis and Habitat serving South and Southeast Minneapolis. Since 1993, Twin Cities Habitat has served nearly two thousand families facing the prospect of foreclosure.

The Bush Foundation was created by a long time 3M executive and his wife, Archibald and Edyth Bush. In nearly fifty years, its support to charitable, scientific, literary, and educational efforts has totaled more than $450 million.

charity. (No stranger to civic responsibility, the Dayton family had also created a charitable foundation back in 1918.) Other companies followed Dayton's lead and joined the "Five Percent Club," as it was then known. In 1976, the Minneapolis Chamber of Commerce assumed control of the program, changing its name to Keystone and recognizing both five percent and two percent donors. From the initial membership of 23 Minnesota companies, the roster has grown to 258 participants by the year 2000, encompassing businesses of all sizes and industry sectors.

To administer their donations, many companies have created foundations and corporate-giving programs. In fact, Minnesota currently has more than one thousand foundations and corporate giving programs, awarding an estimated $734 million to non-profit organizations in 1999. The list of top Minnesota corporate grantmakers reads like a who's who of Twin Cities companies: Target, General Mills, U.S. Bancorp, Cargill, Medtronic, 3M, and The St. Paul Companies, among others.

Target, General Mills, and U.S. Bancorp also appeared in *Worth Magazine's* 2001 list of the nation's top 50 corporate philanthropists. The Target Foundation, supported by the sales from the company's Target, Marshall Fields (formerly Dayton's), and Mervyn's Stores, is projecting more than $80 million in giving for the current year, in support of local social service and arts programs. During the past five years, General Mills reports it has provided more than $171 million in donations and contributions, including over 77 million pounds of food for those in need. And in the last decade,

U.S. Bancorp has donated more than $150 million in grants to affordable housing, economic development, education, and cultural organizations.

In addition to monetary contributions, Twin Cities business people also take active roles in civic improvement, serving on non-profit boards and training leaders of community organizations. Many companies also have instituted programs that facilitate volunteerism among their employees to address community concerns. Minneapolis even has an organization formed by several local chief executives to promote the concept of good corporate citizenship. Known as the Center for Ethical Business Cultures, the 20-year-old group uses seminars, research, and networking to encourage companies to hold themselves to a higher standard.

The number of foundations in Minnesota, corporate and private, grew at a record pace during the 1990s. According to the Foundation Center in New York, the state now ranks thirteenth in total foundation giving. Interestingly, the two most generous private foundations in Minnesota were both founded in 1953 by employees of the 3M Company. Former president and chief executive William L. McKnight, with his wife Maude, formed The McKnight Foundation to strengthen communities, families, and individuals, and contribute to arts, environment, and research groups. Far and away the largest private foundation in the state, it annually awards about $77 million in grants. The Bush Foundation also was created by a longtime 3M executive and his wife, Archibald and Edyth Bush. In nearly fifty years, its support to charitable,

Former president and chief executive of the 3M Company, William L. McKnight, with his wife Maude, formed The McKnight Foundation to strengthen communities, families, and individuals, and contribute to arts, environment, and research groups. Far and away the largest private foundation in the state, it annually awards about $77 million in grants.

scientific, literary, and educational efforts has totaled more than $450 million.

Of course, not all charitable activity in the Twin Cities comes from the business community. Citizens of Minneapolis and St. Paul regularly get involved with worthy causes through volunteer efforts, canvassing neighborhoods and taking part in fund-raising walks, charity balls and events, and organizations like Habitat for Humanity. According to the National Center of Charitable Statistics, Minnesotans rank fifteenth in individual giving.

The high quality of life for which the Twin Cities is so revered is directly attributable to the caring and compassion of the people who live and work here. More than the beauty of our park system, the vibrant arts and culture, or the gleaming downtown skyscrapers, it is the people who make the Twin Cities such a wonderful place to live. ■

Mayo Foundation is a charitable, not-for-profit organization based in Rochester, Minn. Its mission is to provide the best care to every patient every day through integrated clinical practice, education and research. Around the turn of the century, Dr. Charlie and Dr. Will Mayo organized medical professionals in a new way to better care for patients. They created a system that allowed doctors to take the time to thoroughly investigate patient problems and to quickly and easily get help from other specialists. Patients flocked to the Mayos because of their ability to find answers to their problems. Doctors, too, came to observe and learn at "the Mayo's clinic."

Part 2

PARTNERS IN PROGRESS

PricewaterhouseCoopers

As world markets expand beyond national borders, businesses are operating with a broader vision for growth and development. The international professional services firm of PricewaterhouseCoopers has been helping businesses, large and small, reach their full potential and meet the challenges that this new environment presents. It utilizes a vast pool of talent and resources to offer expertise, industry knowledge, and cultural experience to its diverse clientele.

Through a strategic merger in 1998, PwC became the world's largest professional services firm with a network of 150,000 professionals across six continents. The Twin Cities office is among the 18 largest in the United States. It specializes in audit, tax, and advisory services with additional services offered through PwC's global offices. Its staff of 29 partners and 400 employees serve clients in the five-state Midwest region across a range of industries, including banking, insurance, agriculture, manufacturing, wholesale

Barb Marshall (left), CFO of Parasole Restaurant Holdings, is at Manny's Steakhouse in Minneapolis. Manny's, which is listed among the top 10 steakhouses in the country and is owned by Parasole, is managed by Randy Stanley (center). Ellen Valde (right) is a partner in PwC's middle market advisory services practice and the engagement partner on Parasole.

and retail, technology, and energy. Many companies in those industries choose PwC for its far-reaching abilities and expertise, including *Fortune* 500 corporations, small businesses, middle-market businesses, and fast-growing new companies.

"What sets us apart is the attitude that we take to our clients, cultivating long-term relationships with the desire to help them solve their business problems, then having the people, products, and methodologies to get the job done," says Mark Chronister, PwC Office Managing Partner.

PwC fosters a philosophy of superior service and value for its clients. Several methodologies are in place to help meet those objectives. The firm has developed an overall comprehensive service approach called ECLIPSE, meaning Engage Clients/Lead Implementation of Plan/Surpass Expectations. It involves dialoguing with key members of an organization and developing a client expectations document that serves as a roadmap for the client service team. This has helped PwC ensure, and very often exceed, client satisfaction.

The firm's larger clients are also enrolled in a senior partner review program. In an effort to go beyond the client expectations document, a PwC senior partner meets regularly with key executives of the company to review the service process and current issues related to their expectations. Clients have found the review program to be an added value that differentiates PwC from other firms.

Structure of the organization and its services

PwC has several unique strengths that greatly benefit its clients. First, it is structured by industry, which allows the firm to develop expertise in the geographic locations it serves. The Midwest region has a challenging and diverse base of industries—both established and emerging or growing. The Minneapolis office maintains relationships with a variety of venture capitalists who share an interest in the potential this region offers. Many of PwC's clients have found these relationships to be a valuable resource to aid their growth and development plans.

A second strength is PwC's enormous pool of resources available in the United States and around the globe. These resources help clients with the business issues multinational companies face. Many of the firm's Midwest clients have accessed the expertise of PwC's international offices whose staffs have the cultural background, knowledge and resources to assist them with their global marketing strategies.

In addition to its resources, PwC offers clients expertise in three primary lines of service: tax, assurance, and business advisory.

Ward Hamm (right), a partner in PwC's financial services industry group, is the engagement partner for US Bancorp. He is shown here with Richard Davis, a vice chairman of USB, at the company's headquarters.

Tax Services

Helping clients optimize their tax position is one of the tax group's main objectives. It has built an integrated worldwide network of professionals who are experts in the tax issues that businesses face daily. That global reach enables the Minneapolis office to provide unmatched tax resources and high-level, efficient service. Its tax division offers five key areas of service.

- *International Tax Services ITS)*

    PwC's ITS Group provides a full range of international services including international tax structuring, cash repatriation planning, utilization of foreign tax credits, and entity classification. The ITS group issues updates to clients on a regular basis through monthly Tax Alerts.

- *State and Local Tax (SALT)*

    The firm's SALT Practice creates maximum value for its clients by providing comprehensive and coordinated planning for state and local tax minimization. Its state tax professionals specialize in the areas of income/franchise, sales and use, property, unemployment, abandoned and unclaimed properties, credits and incentives, excise, and other state and local taxes.

- *Global Transfer Pricing Services*

    The Global Transfer Pricing Services Group includes prominent economists, lawyers, and tax consultants. Blending their skills, experience, and resources, PwC has developed one of the foremost strategic planning services available. The group assists clients in developing a flexible, achievable, successful strategy that will transform their transfer pricing issues into a competitive advantage.

- *Transaction Support*

    The Transaction Support Tax Group consults with clients on structuring corporate transactions: mergers, acquisitions, joint ventures, divestitures, spin-offs, carve-outs, reorganizations, restructurings, management buyouts, buy/sell agreements, and other transactions. PwC's tax specialists work with clients on all phases of deal planning, tax structuring, financings, valuations, and negotiations. They also consult on hundreds of transactions every year, providing independent and objective advice, as well as industry-specific knowledge that can make all the difference to a successful deal.

- *Washington National Tax Services (WNTS)*

    The WNTS office is widely recognized as the preeminent tax consulting group among the Big Four. On a retainer basis, PwC serves as a Washington tax office for more than 150 major corporations, including half of the *Fortune* 100's largest

The Minneapolis office of PwC hires 25 interns annually. The interns get a taste of the challenges, excitement, and camaraderie of life at PwC.

Mike Brandmeyer (left), a senior manager in the assurance and business advisory services practice, is pictured with Dan Arndt, 3M Company staff vice president and general auditor (center), and Jim Goodwin (right), who is PwC's 3M Company engagement partner.

companies. A team of WNTS industry specialists monitors legislative and regulatory developments of special interest to each client. PwC prepares an in-depth analysis of these developments and recommends strategic tax planning ideas to reduce the tax effects.

Assurance Services

PwC provides full-service audited financial statements built on a technology-driven foundation that is unmatched by any other firm. The firm has developed an interview methodology to review audits among partners, managers, and staff, and create an understanding among them that assures quality on a real-time basis. Audit team members are equipped with laptop computers so they can review current audit documentation at any time. The technology also allows instant communication and speeds the audit process for clients.

Business Advisory Services

Another unique service at PwC is its Global Risk Management Services (GRMS). GRMS helps clients manage

their risks through all economic and market cycles. It focuses on such areas as privacy and security, compliance with governmental regulations, managing financial, operational, systems, and strategic risks, and provides support to audit teams. PwC studies issues from the client's perspective, and assesses their needs in their current environment to better help them meet their goals.

The audit group also provides Transaction Services as a core part of mergers, acquisitions, divestitures, joint ventures, spin-offs, and strategic alliances.

Employee Base and Corporate Atmosphere

PwC is proud of the programs it has developed to serve its worldwide base of employees. One of its many goals was to raise the number of women partners and managers in its branch offices. The Minneapolis office was one of the first to develop a program to meet that goal. It has created networking circles by which manager-level women meet monthly to discuss the challenges women face in the industry and marketplace, and recommend the changes necessary to help them succeed.

The firm has also implemented such changes as flexible work schedules and other accommodations to assist all of its employees through their life cycles from raising children to retirement. In 2001, PwC was rated one of the top places to work by *Working Woman Magazine*, which was the first time a large professional services firm won that honor.

PwC makes a concerted effort to hire people from a variety of backgrounds, and celebrates the diversity of its employee base. It seeks talent from all geographic regions and regularly transfers employees in from other offices who have expertise in specific areas.

PwC employees enjoy the opportunity to transfer to various offices around the world, and the Minneapolis office holds particular appeal. Many transfer employees choose to stay here after experiencing the Twin Cities' vibrant metropolitan area, which offers numerous parks, lakes, and four-season recreational opportunities, as well as a reputable performing arts selection, museums, professional sports, and other entertainment venues.

In an effort to reach out to college students, PwC has created a coveted internship program that offers a career-building start. The firm recruits from local, regional, and national colleges and universities. Interns find the quality of work, professionalism, and company atmosphere to be extremely beneficial as they form their career goals.

Community Service

PwC employees and partners are very involved in community affairs, supporting many charities financially or with volunteer time. Employees regularly participate in fundraising events for United Way, Junior Achievement, Habitat for Humanity, The City, Inc., The Greater Minneapolis Crisis Nursery, and also work with Best Prep to help provide students with the knowledge and skills necessary to face the economic challenges of the future. PwC partners and employees also serve community organizations, such as Minnesota Society of Certified Public Accountants, Minnesota Private College Council, Minnesota Business Partnership, and Minnesota Chamber of Commerce.

Future Growth

PwC is committed to growing the industries it serves locally while operating in a global marketplace. The firm foresees a future in its industry that is more accountable to the public and corporate world, and is committed to rebuilding the trust that has been compromised.

To that end, PwC's CEO, Samuel A. DiPiazza, has laid out a bold plan to reform corporate reporting globally in a new book entitled, *Building Public*

Trust: The Future of Corporate Reporting. DiPiazza proposes establishing a standard of practice in the corporate reporting supply chain that is based on a spirit of transparency, a culture of accountability and individual integrity. He has developed a three-tiered model of corporate transparency whose foundation is a single, global GAAP that is principles-based, not rules-based. The second tier offers industry-based standards for measuring and reporting performance, and the third, company-specific information, such as company value drivers. DiPiazza and PwC plan to bring these ideas and proposals to the public square and advocate for change in the industry. ∎

Mark Chronister, managing partner of PwC's Minneapolis office.

Augsburg College

ugsburg College blossomed from a small seminary in 1868, to become a liberal arts college with international appeal. Located in the midst of one of the nation's largest immigrant populations, in the heart of two cosmopolitan communities, the college has become part of the social, historical, and cultural fabric of the Cedar-Riverside and Seward neighborhoods that adjoin its campus, as well as the city that grew up around it.

Affiliated with the Evangelical Lutheran Church in America, Augsburg is the only private liberal arts college based in Minneapolis. Located just east of downtown Minneapolis, the campus is surrounded by theatres, shops and ethnic restaurants, biking and jogging trails along the nearby Mississippi River, and major sports and shopping venues. Many of the faculty and students reside in the local neighborhoods and are actively involved in committees and associations.

The college not only provides a rigorous education based in the liberal arts and rooted in the Christian faith, it instills life-long learning by emphasizing practical experience, work-ready

Augsburg College's extended metropolitan setting is viewed as an extended campus where students can engage in real-world experiences.
© Augsburg College

skills, broad perspectives, and strong ethics. Coupled with that is a commitment to service that is embedded in the curriculum and campus culture where students are encouraged to live out their vocation and use their gifts to serve others. It is this "Augsburg Experience" that alumni consistently rate as a key factor in shaping their lives and careers.

Embracing its Metropolitan Setting

When Augsburg Seminary moved from rural Wisconsin to Minneapolis in 1872, it was an intentional decision to be an urban-based institution, where it could be involved in a thriving community. Throughout the 1900s, the college and its leaders became more entrenched in civic affairs, and gradually made education its societal mission. By 1963, when the seminary moved to St. Paul in a merger with Luther Theological Seminary, the college had redefined its mission as serving the good of society first, while upholding a motto of "Education for Service."

Today it is often difficult to tell where Augsburg ends and the community begins. The college's metropolitan setting is viewed as an extended campus where students can engage in real world experiences. It is consistently rated as one of the best colleges in the nation that prepares students for the "real world." The college credits the city and its resources for opportunities, such as internships at 3M, Medtronic, and other prominent corporations, as well as the varied businesses in downtown Minneapolis. The city's theatre, music, and art institutions, vast network of non-profit organizations, and government agencies also have provided tremendous opportunities for students majoring in social work, the arts, or public affairs. More than 60 percent of Augsburg students participate in internships and service-learning projects that combine classroom theory with practical experience, and Augsburg faculty have received national awards and recognition for their model service-learning programs.

Service-Based Academic Excellence

Augsburg is a national leader in community-service learning. It is truly a distinguishing factor of the college and has earned it an enviable national reputation. Students learn from and about the community and society by participating in service experiences integrated into Augsburg courses and campus activities. The goal of the program is to build a continuum of community involvement that begins even before classes start for incoming freshmen. First-year students traditionally spend a half-day in service projects around the city the day before classes begin, and a new grant program has allowed for expansion of this community involvement through the entire first semester.

The service-learning program involves partnerships with over 25 community organizations, primarily in the Cedar-Riverside neighborhood. Augsburg students, as well as many faculty and staff, participate in elementary schools, community centers, neighborhood shelters, and churches, and are engaged in researching a variety of community programs to offer analysis and solutions.

One of Augsburg's close community partners is nearby Cedar-Riverside Community School. This public charter school serves a student body largely made up of immigrants who reside in the community. Most of them cannot speak English and are struggling to assimilate in a new country. Each semester, more than 40 Augsburg students spend one to three hours per week at the school as student teachers, tutors, and special projects coordinators. In turn, they learn about the immigrants' diverse cultures and their unique needs in the area of language and work-readiness.

Curriculum

A strong regional institution with a growing national reputation, the college offers undergraduate programs in more than 50 majors and concentrations on both a day and weekend schedule, as well as four graduate programs. It also maintains a branch campus in Rochester, Minn. The college's 3,000 students come from all areas of the United States, and from more than 40 countries. The college has more than 18,000 alumni, among them a United States congressman, Martin Sabo, and his daughter, Minnesota state senator, Julie Sabo, as well as Bishop Herb Chilstrom, former presiding bishop of the ELCA, now retired.

While the college has many outstanding departments, several have achieved special recognition for their programs and opportunities.

Augsburg has one of the strongest undergraduate physics programs available in a private liberal arts setting. It provides varied research opportunities and practical experience in the sciences outside the normal curriculum. For over 25 years, Augsburg has had a research partnership with NASA and the National Science Foundation through grants awarded to faculty members. NASA's Space Grant funding has enabled Augsburg to support an array of public education programs focusing on space science research and exploration. The program promotes educational outreach, teaching, and research in engineering, mathematics, and science fields that support NASA's Strategic Enterprises.

Augsburg was also the first purely undergraduate institution to be linked to NASA's Space Physics Analysis Network (SPAN), now part of the worldwide Internet

Physics and math major Ryan Cobian received a Goldwater Scholarship, one of the premier undergraduate awards nationwide in math, science, and engineering. Augsburg undergraduates conduct on-campus research in space and atmospheric sciences through the College's 20-year relationship with NASA and the National Science Foundation. © Eric Stenbakken

For as long as she can remember, Kelly Duncan has wanted to be a teacher. Now in her student teaching, the education major is grateful for the lessons learned through Augsburg College's hands-on approach in the community. "From my first course on, we spent lots of time in schools," said the Brooklyn Park, Minnesota, native. "That turned out to be the best preparation I could have had." Kelly especially likes working with children who don't seem to fit in. "Often the problem is really a learning disability, something I've had to deal with myself." Augsburg is helping the soon-to-be elementary teacher pursue her dreams. © Eric Stenbakken

computer networking system. The physics department provides opportunities to conduct research through other systems as well, including supercomputers at the National Center for Atmospheric Research, and at remote locations, such as ground-based observatories in Canada, Greenland, and Antarctica. Undergraduates can also obtain employment at Twin Cities firms involved in electronics, optics, biomedical or civil engineering, and space manufacturing technology through the college's Cooperative Education Office.

In the area of education, Minnesota is well served by the college. It is one of two top producers of teachers for K-12 education, and many education students participate in tutoring and student teaching in Twin Cities schools. The education department is committed to developing educational leaders who will serve the diverse classroom with knowledge, ethical practice, reflective thinking, and effective collaboration. Always on the "cutting edge," the department also has embarked on a program to promote the use of technology across the curriculum in both preparing teachers and in K-12 classrooms.

Augsburg's music and art programs offer students unique learning opportunities, thanks to an outstanding faculty and the culturally rich Twin Cities. Music majors and non-majors have access to performances and master classes given by the Minnesota Orchestra, St. Paul Chamber Orchestra, Minnesota Opera, and the Schubert Club, and art majors draw inspiration and ideas through the college's

association with numerous art galleries and museums. Internships and study abroad programs are also available, and encourage students to grow in the professional world.

As a faith-based institution, Augsburg College also nurtures vocations through its youth and family ministry major. It provides the preparation needed for careers working with children, youth, and families in congregations, social agencies, and other Christian organizations. Students are not only given the academic background, but practical experience for ministerial positions or further study in seminaries.

For students seeking a high-level academic experience, Augsburg designed a nationally recognized Honors Program that blends an enriched course of study, individual support, and a community of students committed to scholarship. The Honors Program challenges students to think, question, and examine ideas in new ways, and is a valuable asset for job placement and graduate school. Many honors graduates have gone on to Harvard, Yale, Princeton, and other top graduate school programs.

International Studies Programs

Augsburg upholds international studies as a vital part of an education that prepares students for work in the increasingly global marketplace. It has been ahead of the trend toward global education, implementing a variety of study abroad programs through its Office of International Programs. Its unique International Partners Program offers high-quality learning opportunities for students in business, education, and social work. Based on reciprocal agreements with Norway and Germany, Augsburg students can complete part of their coursework at these participating educational institutions, and students from those institutions can study at Augsburg. The program also offers students practical experiences in Norwegian and German businesses, schools, and social agencies—often in paid positions.

Augsburg's Center for Global Education has been offering study programs in Central America, Africa, and Mexico since 1982. The program integrates academics, cultural interaction, and travel, and draws college students and adults from all over the country.

Athletics Blend With Academic Achievement

Augsburg College takes special pride in the academic achievements of its "Auggie" athletes. On an annual basis, Augsburg athletes in all sports have received GTE Academic All-District and Academic All-America awards, among the highest honors given to athletes for achievements on the field and the classroom. Auggies have not only won championships in wrestling, track and field, basketball, hockey, and football, but have consistently achieved grade point averages that rank among the highest in the nation.

Outreach Programs

Augsburg has a higher-than-average percentage of students of color, and more programs designed to support students of color than any other Minnesota college. Included in that is a successful American Indian Program that primarily serves the nation's largest urban population of Native American Indians located just a mile off campus.

Since the 1980s, Augsburg has been the state's largest provider of weekend undergraduate programs designed for an adult student base. It is a means for men and women to earn a baccalaureate degree while maintaining a job, changing careers, gaining professional skills, or fulfilling a personal goal. The Weekend College program serves 1,200 students enrolled in 17 majors, and continues to grow in demand. Augsburg also provides five graduate programs in social work, nursing, leadership, education, and a physician assistant program that has an enrollment demand four times the program's capacity.

Augsburg College athletes have earned "All American" honors in intercollegiate hockey, football, wrestling, track and field, and softball. Augsburg competes in the Minnesota Intercollegiate Athletic Conference whose teams frequently vie for national titles. © Tom Dahlin

Future Growth

Augsburg's future is very much entwined in the future of the city. Its current leadership believes that partnerships among academic institutions, city, and corporate groups are essential for the economic development and growth of the entire community. In addition to expanding its facilities and curriculum, the college will continue to forge partnerships in the local and global community, while maintaining the motto of "Education for Service" as its primary motivation. ■

Mall of America

The Mall of America is recognized globally as the largest retail and entertainment complex in the United States. A destination without peer, this world-class shopping mecca has hosted 390 million visitors since it opened in August 1992, and is setting new standards for shopping and entertainment in the retail industry.

Built in Bloomington, the Twin Cities' largest suburb, the Mall is conveniently located along the (highway) "494 Strip," where visitors have access to numerous hotels and businesses, major freeways, and the Minneapolis/St. Paul International Airport. Over 40 million people visit the Mall each year, which is more than the annual visitors to Disneyland, Graceland, and the Grand Canyon combined. In addition to free parking, there is no entrance fee to the Mall or its family entertainment epicenter, Camp Snoopy Amusement Park.

When ground first broke on the Mall 13 years ago, Minnesotans were reserved about such an aggressive project.

North Entrance to Mall of America.

Mall of America's East Wing, "East Broadway."

But when the doors opened, word quickly spread about its unique and impressive stature. To give an idea of its magnitude, the Mall could hold two of the world's largest pyramids or 258 Statues of Liberty. Shoppers soon discovered that to browse in every store would take multiple visits. Despite any initial reservations, the Mall enjoys the preeminent position today as the nation's most visited destination.

The Mall has been a boon for Minnesota tourism, and specifically the Twin Cities. It ranks ahead of New York, Chicago, and Las Vegas for family destinations. The two most popular seasons for visitors are June-July-August and the holiday seasons of November and December. Despite the state's temperamental weather, the 4.2 million-square-foot complex is a comfortable indoor paradise. Just the sheer number of daily visitors, combined with miles of lights, generates enough warmth to heat the entire complex even on the coldest days.

The cumulative economic impact on the state of Minnesota has been an impressive $12.4 billion dollars in the last decade, or nearly $1.6 billion annually. Money spent at the Mall flows into the surrounding community. For every dollar spent there, another two to three dollars is spent outside the mall for gas, lodging, food, and other amenities. Approximately 80 percent of the Mall's economic impact has come from out-of-state visitors. Tourism from outside a 150-mile radius accounts for almost 40 percent of the Mall's traffic and of that, six percent are international visitors.

Retail Success

The Mall of America houses more than 520 stores on three retail levels. A fourth level is reserved for nightlife and entertainment. Dozens of specialty stores line the avenues connecting four major department stores located at each corner of the Mall: Bloomingdale's, Macy's, Nordstrom, and Sears.

Shoppers have one-stop access to a large selection of shops, including upscale fashion retailers, children's, teen, and bargain apparel, accessories and shoes, sports and outdoor gear, music and videos, books, toys, home furnishings, unique gifts, and other businesses. The Mall serves up a culinary banquet with 86 eating establishments, offering everything from fast food to fine dining and ethnic cuisine.

The Mall has helped hundreds of entrepreneurs to grow their businesses from small kiosks, or carts, into successful retail stores. Its Retail Development Program (RDP) looks for new and unique retails concepts to compliment the already unique shopping experience. The person who can pull together a theme or product that is hot or new is invited to present the idea to the RDP staff, who works closely with the entrepreneur to take the idea to the Mall marketplace.

RDP offers a professional staff to help with promotion and marketing inside and outside the Mall. On site designers help set up a kiosk or custom-design a store that will connect with customers immediately. It also has a temporary lease program that many small retailers utilize to test out a concept or location before committing to permanent leases.

Liten Hus, a Scandinavian lifestyle store, opened in 1999 with a temporary lease. After moving around a few years, it settled on a permanent location that has worked very well.

"It's a real good way for a small retailer like us to find out what kind of space we need, what location we need and whether or not being in the Mall will be successful for us," says Susan Nyhusmoen, owner of Liten Hus.

More than 100 stores in the complex are unique to Minnesota. The Rocky Mountain Chocolate Factory was one of the original retailers at the Mall. It had tried several times to find a location in Minnesota that made sense for its product. The success at the Mall has helped Rocky Mountain Chocolate Factory become a recognizable name, and it has since expanded to other Minnesota locations.

"Location is very critical. It's got to be the right mixture of people to make it a success," says Gail Stein, the franchise owner. "Unique shops work here because people want to come to the Mall to get that stuff while they're here. It's hard to go somewhere else in Minnesota and compete with what we have here."

Two other unique tenants are QVC @ the Mall and Apple Computer. Shoppers can browse the 2,500-square-foot QVC store and purchase the products that made this home shopping powerhouse famous. Apple Computer is the only retail store in the state.

Mall of America's West Wing, "West Market."

Mall of America's South Wing, "South Avenue."

Underwater Adventures Observation Tunnel.

It hosts 30 adventurous rides and attractions that operate year-round. The PEANUTS Gang—Linus, Lucy, Charlie Brown, Sally, and Snoopy—make periodic appearances. Park visitors can also shop at souvenir stores, win prizes at the game centers, and eat at themed restaurants. Since the Mall opened, Camp Snoopy has provided 75 million rides.

Equally impressive is Underwater World, a 1.2 million-gallon aquarium where visitors can view more than 3,000 species of living sea creatures from a 14-foot tunnel that takes them through the aquarium. Sharks, stingrays, giant sea turtles, moray eels, puffer fish, and hundreds of beautiful tropical species can be viewed from just inches away. A colorful rainbow reef, exotic animals, and shark coves are just part of the visit. Before entering the aquarium, visitors also get a taste of the Minnesota North woods in a stroll that offers close-up views of its native fish and wildlife.

The LEGO® Imagination Center attracts guests of all ages to its four-story showplace. More than 30 full-size

Unique Events

More than 3,500 couples have been married at the Mall since 1982, many at the Chapel of Love. Perhaps one of the most unique marriages that made international news was that of David Weinlick. Based on recommendations from his closest friends, he chose his wife from a number of women who sought his hand in a contest at the Mall.

Many performers and new talent eye the Mall for its built-in traffic and as a venue to reach Midwest audiences sandwiched between New York and Los Angeles. It has hosted numerous celebrities and performers as well as Hollywood filmmakers. The Mall was a site for two movies, *Jingle All the Way* and *Mighty Ducks*, and the site of the World Premier of *Ice Age*.

Family Entertainment

Some of the most impressive features of the Mall are the family attractions that draw thousands of visitors every day. A most remarkable sight is the seven-acre Camp Snoopy indoor theme park-the nation's largest-that rises up the very center of the complex. The spacious and open-air park is visible from every level of the Mall, marked by a two-story high Snoopy. Its outdoor design features 30,000 live plants, 400 live trees, and 20,000 ladybugs that provide natural pest control. More than a mile of skylights allows 70 percent of the park's natural light to stream in.

Mall of America's North Wing, "North Garden."

animated and interactive LEGO models are on display, including dinosaurs, ships, astronauts, and a blimp that was made with 138,240 LEGO bricks. A play station is set up for children, and a store offers a full range of LEGO products.

Finally, guests can learn how cereal is made and take home a personalized package at the new General Mills Cereal Adventure. It features the Cheerios Play Park and Lucky Charms' Magical Forest among other attractions, based on the products of the Minnesota-based company.

Community and Charitable Giving

The Mall of America has not only had a tremendous impact on the local economy, it also partners with numerous charitable organizations to help raise millions of dollars and community awareness for various causes. Mall of America and Northwest Airlines have partnered to host the annual "Thanksgiving Walk for Hunger." The Juvenile Diabetes Foundation raises a significant amount of money each year in its "Walk for the Cure" and St. Judes Hospital had tremendous fundraising success in its first 2001 radiothon.

The Mall has also established a Foundation for Youth non-profit organization that helps the development of youth, and provides scholarships to college-bound students.

Future Growth and Development

In 1992, Mall of America transformed the retail and entertainment world and created a destination without equal. Now we are ready to once again set new standards in shopping and entertainment, and lead the retail industry in the new millennium.

Mall of America is poised to further broaden and enhance its appeal to both domestic and international visitors as its developers are well into the process of defining a vision that will incorporate a combination of synergistic uses that may include:
• Premier hotels on site
• Office complex/business center with conference facilities
• Unique new retail offerings
• Popular destination restaurants
• Recreational/fitness/spa facilities
• Entertainment/cultural attractions
While still in the planning stages, Mall of America's Phase II concepts will display a lifestyle-oriented, progressive, and innovative personality that will complement the existing shops and attractions at Mall of America. The Phase II mixed-use complex is zoned for up to 5.7 million square feet of new development and will be built on 42 acres of adjacent property to the north of Mall of America on the old site of the Met Center. A bridge will also be constructed to link Phase I and Phase II.

Announcements of committed concepts and tenants could begin as early as fall 2002. ■

Camp Snoopy's Kite Eating Tree.

Camp Snoopy's Skyscraper Ferris Wheel.

Allianz Life Insurance Company of North America

llianz Life Insurance Company of North America is recognized by industry leaders as one of the most progressive, innovative life insurance companies in the country. It leads the industry in many areas, among them creating value-added products that protect its customers not only upon death, but also in life. The Golden Valley-based company is today taking the life insurance market to a new generation of service and products that is unprecedented.

The company began in 1896 as North American Life Association, founded by Henry Little of Minneapolis. In 1912 it merged with North American Casualty Company to form North American Life and Casualty (NALAC) and became a national industry innovator. NALAC was acquired by Allianz AG of Munich, Germany, in 1979. Allianz AG is one of the leading financial enterprises in the world, operating in over 70 countries.

In 1993, NALAC was renamed Allianz Life Insurance Company of North America (Allianz Life). Today it is a $24 billion dollar enterprise that operates in all 50 states, the District of Columbia, and Guam. The company writes in excess of $5.0 billion in premiums annually and continues to lead U.S. sales of equity indexed annuity products. It ranks number five in fixed annuity products, and number seven in the life reinsurance market. It is among the top 10 in sales of long term care products, and in the top 25 in variable annuity products. It also maintains a significant presence in the healthcare reinsurance market, and boasts a retail broker/dealer dedicated to independent registered

Allianz Life Insurance headquarters building in Golden Valley, Minnesota.

Mark Zesbaugh, CEO of Allianz Life.

representatives. Along with its continually increased market share, Allianz Life maintains some of the highest ratings issued by the A.M. Best Co. and Standard & Poor's.

The corporate structure is comprised of five primary business units. They include the Allianz Life Individual Insurance Group, USAllianz Investor Services, LLC®, Allianz Re, Allianz Healthcare Re, and USAllianz Securities. The company is represented by one of the largest distribution networks in the country, with over 200,000 independent agents, registered representatives, and financial planners nationwide. Allianz Life serves the individual market with a variety of life insurance products, annuities and long-term care products. The institutional market is served by Allianz Re, the seventh largest life reinsurance provider in the United States, and Allianz Healthcare Re, offering products to Health Maintenance Organizations and to companies that want a means to fund their own health plans.

Allianz Life individual insurance products focus on three key elements of asset management: asset accumulation products, asset protection products, and asset distribution products. The categories are intertwined and offer a variety of products for all stages of life. One of its core business strategies is to be a leader in asset distribution products, a segment of the market that is expected to expand consistent with changing consumer demand.

Targeting the Future

The company has experienced a tremendous amount of growth in recent years. From fiscal year 1999 to 2001, its earned premiums grew from $3.3 billion to nearly $4.5 billion, and are expected to exceed $7 billion in 2002. Within three years by 2001, its workforce had grown 50 percent to nearly 2,000 employees. Allianz Life moved into a newly built corporate headquarters in Golden Valley in August 2001.

Much of its success can be attributed to its focus on the future-targeting consumer needs based on what's coming as opposed to living in what was. Allianz Life foresaw a need to redesign the way life insurance policies were written and distributed. The company augmented its product portfolio, which placed it in a strategic position to lead the industry beyond traditional life insurance.

Allianz Life Executive Management Team (left to right) Denise Blizil, chief administrative officer (CAO); Mark Zesbaugh, CEO; Chuck Kavitsky, president; Gabby Matzdorff, CFO; and Suzanne Pepin, chief legal counsel.

In recent decades, medical technology has advanced to the degree that people are living longer than ever before in history. Illnesses that in the past were fatal are today easily survived. The impact on the economy and culture is tremendous. It is not uncommon for people to live 20 to 30 years beyond retirement. Allianz Life recognized the necessity to not only help people protect against the economic cost of dying, but to protect against the economic cost of living.

One example of how Allianz Life has responded to this major demographic change is the introduction of the first redesigned product in its asset accumulation category at the start of 2002. Allianz Classic LifeFund is a new generation life insurance product that not only pays if the policyholder dies, but also pays upon some more immediate risks—unforeseen life events, such as accidents, specified critical illnesses, or disabilities—that can cause serious financial setbacks. LifeFund is possibly the first life insurance policy to offer a pool of money that policyholders can access in the event of one of these setbacks, to provide income when it is most needed. It also provides an option to elect retirement income if the policyholder elects to do so after a certain

age or length of policy. Simply put, Allianz Life describes LifeFund as the first life insurance policy that makes you the beneficiary.

LifeFund is a major shift in how life insurance customers can manage their assets while they are living. Allianz Life expects other companies to follow their lead; thereby changing the face of the life insurance industry. In the meantime, the company expects to double its production within a year, with exponential growth to follow.

Corporate Atmosphere

Allianz Life fosters a philosophy of big company stability with personal relationships. It has a corporate attitude that puts people first. The open structure helps create a culture that values the individual. Its approach to employees is as real people who are defining the company and leading it into the future.

"There are no silos in our business; we share information with each other," says Chuck Kavitsky, President of Allianz Life. "There's an understanding that we all work together. Especially when you're growing so fast, there's nothing more important than the individual."

That attitude is passed on to its customers. Among its competitors, Allianz Life has a reputation for personal service that is unmatched. In the age of voice messaging,

e-mail, and Internet communication, Allianz Life connects its customers with real people who are set on building long-term relationships.

"Products and programs can be copied, but great people cannot be copied. The people of Allianz Life are the greatest competitive advantage we have," says Mark Zesbaugh, Allianz Life CEO.

Kavitsky also credits the solid ethics of Midwesterners for the company's reputation, and believes in tapping into the local base for its employees. "I can think of no better workforce than the Midwest," says Kavitsky. "Any company that comes to Minneapolis will find that the people here really make a difference."

Allianz Life was twice voted one of the 14 Best Places to Work in the Twin Cities by *CityBusiness*. The award is based on employee attitude surveys and company benefits surveys. Of the more than 774 public and private companies and non-profits surveyed, Allianz Life scored the highest in employee attitudes and in the top five in employee benefits. At the heart of the employee attitudes was ownership—employees feel they are given a measure of control over both the direction of the company and their professional growth.

"We invest in people to help them increase their knowledge and develop their professional skills. People develop an ownership of their jobs when they are given the opportunity to advance in their careers," notes Zesbaugh.

Allianz Life created an Employee Council to support and enhance enterprise-wide business initiatives. It manages a monthly employee recognition program called S.O.A.R. (Supporting Ongoing Achievement Recognition). It also conducts a month-long celebration of fun activities each year to recognize employee performance and to build internal relationships, culminating with an annual banquet to recognize both individual employee and team achievements. Every Allianz Life employee is also eligible for incentive compensation based

Zesbaugh attributes the high quality of life in Minneapolis to the involvement of its business community and city residents. "The quality of a community is a direct result of citizen participation in its affairs and corporate support of its mission and goals. The business community of Minneapolis has a long tradition of strong support to the city and to community organizations. We at Allianz Life are proud to be a part of the community and we're committed to doing our part in giving back to the community. Minneapolis is a great place to live and work, and we want to keep it that way." ■

on the company's business results and individual work performance. This approach gives employees a personal stake in meeting company goals.

Charitable Spirit

Its commitment to the Twin Cities community is forthright. Starting with the Executive Management team, community service is embedded in the Allianz Life corporate atmosphere. Employees are actively involved in numerous volunteer activities and charitable donations. Employees are paid for eight hours of community service as a contribution to the Twin Cities area. That program has fostered a spirit of volunteerism by which employees donate hundreds of additional hours to numerous community projects and organizations. They also vote each year on four primary community organizations and charities that will receive designated funds from the company.

In addition to the employee program, the company actively supports charitable causes through corporate giving, providing financial resources to assist many community organizations in fulfilling their mission. The company also sponsors The Allianz Championship, a major SENIOR PGA TOUR golf tournament held in West Des Moines, Iowa, with the proceeds dedicated to community organizations in Iowa.

Minneapolis Regional Chamber of Commerce

*T*he Twin Cities is widely known for having a strong, healthy business climate and a quality of life that differentiates it from other metropolitan regions. The diverse mix of industries has helped the area thrive, even during economic downturns. The Minneapolis Regional Chamber of Commerce has contributed greatly to the region's strength, and is committed to its continued growth and development.

"Since the Chamber was first established in the late 1800s, it has taken great pride in representing the Twin Cities and being a source of its economic prosperity. Today, as the largest regional Chamber in the state of Minnesota, we still focus on the development of existing businesses and the global recruitment of new business to the metropolitan area," said Louise Dickmeyer, Chamber president and CEO.

The MRCC was created to be an effective business organization whose primary goal is to facilitate economic growth through business recruitment, retention, and development in the Minneapolis-St. Paul metropolitan region. It consists of a network of 2,000 member organizations—including Fortune 500 companies, small businesses, and entrepreneurs-from 70 different communities.

Membership in the Minneapolis Regional Chamber has many benefits that exceed local chambers. The Chamber provides its membership with a variety of marketing opportunities and networking events; assists its members with business expansion and development plans by working with regional and state

Minnesota Twins' players Kirby Puckett and Denny Hocking address the chamber membership.

resources; and identifies and promotes members' interests in public policy initiatives at the state and local government.

Chamber councils have been set up to serve the specific interests of the metropolitan region. The Bloomington Airport Council focuses on issues surrounding the airport, hospitality, and transportation as well as localized programming for the city of Bloomington. The Minneapolis Council focuses on issues relevant to the downtown area and specifically the overall city of Minneapolis. The Small Business Council meets the needs of small business members and the issues that affect them.

Positioning the region for growth

The MRCC is positioned to become more effective in addressing regional issues and finding regional solutions to ensure that the business community can grow throughout the entire area. "We are competing with Denver, St. Louis, Seattle, Munich, and Tokyo for businesses and markets that are growing or expanding, and we have all the aspects here that are important to business growth and development," Dickmeyer said.

The Chamber has partnered with other area business organizations and civic leaders in a united effort to advance the business and commercial interests of the area. A key goal is to recruit new businesses to the area, and determine select industries to target its efforts. The Chamber's marketing strategies include positioning the Twin Cities as a viable and robust region to do business, and a vibrant place to live.

Governor Jesse Ventura enjoys himself at a chamber luncheon.

Through its position in the community, the Chamber has identified key public policy issues that are critical to the economic vitality of the metropolitan region. Primarily it focuses on transportation planning that emphasizes system-wide connectedness and efficiency, as well as improvements to the Minneapolis-St. Paul Airport, a crucial strength of the region's business community.

The Chamber favors responsible use of redevelopment tools and capital investments that enhance the overall growth of the regional economy. It supports workforce planning that is responsive to the individual communities, and to the needs of employers and employees. Finally, it supports measures that enhance the quality of life here, including the availability of professional and amateur sports, and a strong performing arts community.

The Chamber also supports policies that help strengthen the quality of healthcare, education, and the environment, fair and responsible tax policies, and use of tax dollars that provide value for the investment.

One of the key economic development issues that the Chamber consistently emphasizes is workforce development. It obtained a grant from the U.S. Department of Labor to create a regional workforce development plan. From that plan, the Chamber conducted a Minneapolis-St. Paul Regional Workforce Training Audit, to better understand what employers need from the region's workforce system. It also developed a Plan for Enhancing Regional Workforce Competence that brought together small, mid-size and large employers as well as regional policy makers to dialog about workforce needs.

In other actions, the Chamber has engaged regional leaders in workforce development efforts through a variety of seminars and programs, including an inter-city visit to Denver with 80 regional civic and business leaders. The Chamber also views education as playing a key role in workforce development. It has partnered with area schools and colleges to develop and promote these workforce initiatives that serve the region's employer and employee base.

"In today's fast-paced economy, every business—regardless of industry or size-wants access to resources that will help them grow," Dickmeyer said. "The Minneapolis Regional Chamber of Commerce provides what every business needs, including access to new markets, professional training, an educated workforce, and a voice in government."

St. Paul Mayor Norm Coleman greets chamber members.

"The MRCC is the only organization in this region that serves the business community, seeks opportunities that strengthen the economic vitality and quality of life in the Minneapolis-St. Paul metropolitan region, and promotes these qualities to the global marketplace."

"This Chamber has been the leader in business and economic development since the 1880s—and we have every intention of keeping it that way." ■

The Minnesota Keystone Program presented the 2001 Honored Company Award to Wells Fargo Minnesota for their contribution to the community. The Minnesota Keystone Program is operated by the Minneapolis Regional Chamber of Commerce.

Fredrikson & Byron, P.A.

*F*redrikson & Byron, P.A. is an international law firm of 170+ attorneys providing legal and business advisory counsel in over 30 subject matters under the areas of Business & Finance, Dispute Resolution & Litigation, Intellectual Property, and Personal Legal Services. The firm serves a diverse client base of publicly and privately held businesses, financial institutions, municipalities, corporations, and nonprofits, ranging in size from entrepreneurs to multi-national companies.

Fredrikson & Byron is based in Minneapolis, and has an office in London, and affiliate offices in Montreal, Toronto, Vancouver, Mexico City, and Warsaw. With its worldwide network of attorneys and advisors, Fredrikson & Byron is a valuable resource to its clients.

Walter J. Wheeler founded the firm in 1948. He was joined by Harold Fredrikson in 1953 and John Byron two years later. Fredrikson & Byron grew steadily, and merged with Wright, West & Diessner in 1984. Today it is one of the Upper Midwest's largest business and trial law firms.

Where Law and Business Meet

As the business landscape has evolved, Fredrikson & Byron has expanded to offer more than legal counsel. Its attorneys often function as business advisors and strategic partners, and have built a reputation as the firm where "law and business meet" by bringing business acumen and entrepreneurial thinking into its service to clients.

It has developed ancillary services through Fredrikson Healthcare Consulting, Ltd., and Fredrikson Human Resources Consulting, Ltd., who provide specific business insights that are vital to the clients' growth and long-term goals.

Service

The firm's attorneys and employees pride themselves on high service standards. They provide counsel to clients throughout the world, and staff key business support services seven days a week.

Diversity

Fredrikson & Byron values diversity in its clients and employees, and is committed to the needs of a diverse community.

The firm offers an annual scholarship to minority law students, and regularly provides pro bono and community services to a wide variety of people, organizations, and projects. It was one of the first law firms in the nation to subscribe to the American Bar Association's Law Firm Challenge, which asks large law firms to contribute at least three percent of their total billable hours each year to work for the public good. Its employees

Fredrikson & Byron's headquarters are located in the 40-story angular tower of Pillsbury Center, located in the heart of Minneapolis, Minnesota.

actively support programs that benefit disadvantaged individuals, and regularly volunteer at schools and charitable organizations throughout the Twin Cities metropolitan area.

Fredrikson & Byron attributes its 50-plus years of success to the dedicated contributions of its attorneys and employees, and looks forward to continued growth and success in the 21st Century. ■

Fredrikson & Byron's main reception area, on the top floor of the Pillsbury Tower.

Carlson Companies

he Twin Cities has a solid business base built by a wealth of entrepreneurs, one of whom established the foundation for today's Carlson Companies, a global corporate leader in the marketing, travel, and hospitality industries. Carlson Companies was started in 1938 by Curtis Carlson, who foresaw the value of relationship marketing before it became a marketing objective of the '90s. More than 60 years ago, he initiated Gold Bond Stamps, a stamps-for-merchandise program that helped grocers and other independent merchants promote their goods and compete for customers.

That simple program evolved into what is today one of the largest privately-held corporations in the country. The enterprise has operations in 140+ countries, and its systemwide brands and services generate more than $19 billion in sales annually. Still grounded on a foundation of relationship marketing, Carlson Companies is headed by Chairman and Chief Executive Officer Marilyn Carlson Nelson, recognized worldwide for her business-leadership acumen.

Carlson Companies provides unparalleled expertise in marketing and travel programs for thousands of corporate customers, including Fortune 1,000 companies worldwide. Carlson Marketing Group®, the world leader in relationship marketing, helps clients improve their sales and profits by designing marketing strategies which build better relationships with their audiences: employees, channel partners, and consumers. Corporate customers also rely on Carlson Wagonlit Travel® to provide travel-management services and a maximum return on investment. The synergy between the two groups offers expertise, convenience, and cost-savings to corporations, while helping them advance their goals in building customer relationships.

Carlson also serves the lifestyles of customers worldwide through well-known brands, including Regent® International Hotels, Radisson® Hotels & Resorts, Country Inns & Suites By Carlson®, Park Plaza® and Park Inn® hotels, T.G.I. Friday's®

Carlson Companies, headquartered west of Minneapolis, is a global leader in relationship marketing, business and leisure travel, and hospitality services.

and Pick Up Stix® restaurants, Radisson Seven Seas Cruises®, and Carlson Wagonlit Travel® Associates.

Carlson's Gold Points Rewards℠ program builds customer loyalty while generously rewarding shoppers with accumulated points that can be redeemed at online and "bricks and mortar" businesses. They include Carlson Companies' hotels, vacation properties, and restaurants, and a variety of program partners' brands at thousands of locations.

Giving Back to the Community

Carlson Companies has been rated one of the top companies in the Twin Cities and the nation. The company has been recognized by *Fortune* and *Working Mother* magazines as one of the best places to work for in America. A champion of community leadership and philanthropy, the company has donated five percent of gross revenues to charity annually, including generous support for the University of Minnesota where Curt Carlson graduated, and the Carlson School of Management. The company also recently initiated the Carlson Volunteer Connection, which connects Carlson employees with volunteer opportunities throughout the Twin Cities.

Carlson Companies' future involves growth through partnerships in related industries, and implementing technology to stay competitive in the global marketplace. ■

Established in 1965, T.G.I. Friday's is credited as being one of the first American casual-dining chains.

Candlewood Suites

Candlewood Suites offers a comfortable stay whether you are a business traveler or on a leisurely vacation.

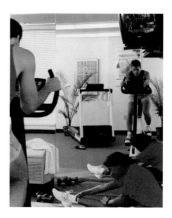

Guests are able to keep their usual exercise routine thanks to the complimentary fitness area.

Candlewood Suites has taken the hotel business to a new level for the business traveler. It provides the conveniences of office and home in a comfortable hotel suite at a tremendous value to its guests.

The hotel offers spacious studio and one-bedroom suites that are fully equipped with a work area and a relaxing living space. Even the smaller studio suites are 33 percent larger than a standard hotel room. Each suite is furnished with an executive desk and chair, queen-size bed, recliner, home entertainment components, and kitchens that include a full size refrigerator with ice maker, stove, microwave, dishwasher, garbage disposal, and cooking utensils. Guests also enjoy two phone lines, low long-distance costs, free local phone calls, 25-cent sodas, free laundry facilities, and a free fitness center. Candlewood Suites provides an on-site convenience store where guests can purchase groceries, toiletries, and other amenities at a price that doesn't gauge them, but is as close to cost as possible.

Jack DeBoor, the founder and brainchild behind the business, created the Residence Inn in the 1970s, which was later sold to Marriott Corporation. His extensive research revealed that business travelers don't like to eat out all the time, preferring instead to make their own meals and eat in. With that in mind, he developed the concept for hotel rooms that feel more like mini apartments.

His corporate philosophy is to be an expert in the hotel business—provide greater value in the hotel room itself by dispensing of costly add-ons, such as restaurants, concierge services, and airport transportation. The concept has been a winner with customers. For four years, Candlewood Suites has had the highest rating of guests who prefer it over other hotel stays.

The company position, "Life on the road at its best," is proven in the quick expansion it has experienced. It has built hotels in every major market in the United States where business travelers frequent. There are currently 103 Candlewood Suites around the country and 15 under construction. Eyeing the Twin Cities as a major business hub, the company built a 134-suite hotel in Richfield in 1998, with convenient access to the airport and Mall of America. Plans are underway to build more Candlewood Suites in other Twin Cities locations.

While its primary focus is the corporate, extended-stay traveler, it also caters to people who are relocating and need a place to stay until a permanent residence is found. Still other guests are leisure travelers who want more than a hotel room. Its mission for all customers is to provide the best possible hotel experience at a good, honest price. ∎

Each suite is furnished with many amenities including a full-size refrigerator, dishwasher, and microwave oven.

Diversified Equities Corporation

The city of Minneapolis has benefited tremendously from the efforts of one downtown developer whose philosophy of "community first" has done much to improve housing in the city. Jon E. Dickerson founded Diversified Equities Corporation (DEC) in 1971. DEC provides safe, clean, affordable housing by developing, managing, and marketing real estate, particularly for disabled and disadvantaged people. The company organizes partnerships to acquire and develop housing in the Minneapolis/St. Paul metro area.

Dickerson grew up in Northeast Minneapolis near his current office. His parents instilled in him a strong work ethic to "do something to improve the community." After a five-year stint selling real estate and limited partnership shares, Dickerson decided to focus on real estate development that could benefit the community. He founded Diversified Equities Corporation and began revitalizing existing buildings. He also began developing new buildings into affordable housing units, a venture that has grown with the increasing demand for such housing. Some of the properties are managed by DEC; others are sold and the profits are used to finance additional real estate projects.

The company, which employs nine people, has completed 14 major housing projects involving over 2,000 apartments, townhouses, and condominiums around the metro area, as well as commercial space. One of DEC's ventures involved the rehabilitation of a turn-of-the-century nursing home near Downtown Minneapolis otherwise headed for the wrecking ball. DEC purchased the empty buildings from the city's development agency, and with financing from Minnesota Housing Finance Agency, adapted them for use as a beautiful

Residents with a wide range of incomes can afford to live at this reborn historically significant property.

71-unit rental apartment community known as Stonehouse Square Apartments.

The company followed the same format to develop a new building where it operates. Holmes-Greenway Housing project is a 50-unit apartment complex, located just across the river from Downtown Minneapolis. It serves a variety of people with special needs and also rents commercial space.

Dickerson has participated in city development for many years and advocates for low income and disadvantaged persons. He has been active at the Chamber of Commerce, the Minnesota Multi-Housing Association, and numerous community groups. His corporation works with the city to reuse sites by resolving zoning issues, planning marketable improvements, and organizing financing solutions. He also manages the programs and procedures necessary to serve the broad range of tenants at his properties.

The need for affordable housing continues to be a complex issue as markets rise and fall, regulatory environments change, and tenant expectations grow. Diversified Equities Corporation's mission to serve the affordable housing market is fueled by an increasing demand and the successful ventures it has already completed. It will continue to provide positive contributions and revitalization solutions to Twin Cities communities. ∎

Affordable townhouses on this reused school site house moderate income families.

Minnesota Technology, Inc.

innesota Technology, Inc. was established in 1991 to contribute to the growth of Minnesota's economy through technology. It helps create a robust Greater Minnesota economy that features a diverse mix of advanced manufacturing and technology-based businesses that provide secure, well-paying jobs. Since its inception, Minnesota Technology, Inc. has served over 4,600 companies and helped the state's economy realize gains of more than $600 million as a direct result of Minnesota Technology, Inc's. products and services.

Minnesota Technology, Inc. helps grow advanced manufacturing and technology-based companies that provide secure, well-paying jobs.

Minnesota Technology, Inc. helps companies create more effective manufacturing processes, improve communications, increase efficiency, expand market opportunities, and develop corporate growth strategies. Business and engineering specialists in 17 locations around the state provide one-on-one consulting to small- and mid-sized companies in five areas: Tech Transfer, IT/Internet-related services, Lean Enterprise, Business Intelligence, and New Product Development. The organization also links Minnesota companies with federal laboratories and researchers at higher-education institutions.

Minnesota Technology, Inc. is the state's premier resource for technology information and trends. It publishes reports, such as *Our Competitive Nature: Minnesota's Technology Economy*, that keep legislators and community leaders informed about issues affecting technology industries and the economy. The organization produces a quarterly magazine, *Minnesota Technology®* magazine, which profiles Minnesota companies and people, and keeps readers up-to-date with trends and innovations. Minnesota Technology, Inc. offers a number of online resources, such as the *Minnesota Technology Directory*, a listing of over 2,000 of Minnesota's technology-driven businesses and the

Manufacturer's Training Resource, a listing of business- and manufacturing-related courses and seminars. Minnesota Technology, Inc. has partnered with Teltech.com to provide a portal to their online research library. Minnesota Technology, Inc. also has information services professionals on staff.

The organization sponsors a number of technology-related events. Through its ongoing Technology Awareness Forums, Minnesota Technology, Inc. has educated hundreds of business leaders about advanced and emerging technologies. It hosts an annual conference intended to stimulate new thinking about economic development among community leaders. Every month at its "Future Visions" forum, outside speakers present on technologies that are changing the world.

Promoting Minnesota's technology community is also a key part of Minnesota Technology, Inc.'s work. In partnership with the Minnesota High Tech Association, Minnesota Technology, Inc. produces the annual Minnesota's Tekne Awards. The awards recognize excellence in innovation, development, commercialization, and management of technology in Minnesota. Recipients represent technology innovators who have made lasting contributions to enhancing the state's quality of life and competitiveness.

Minnesota Technology, Inc. is an invaluable resource for Minnesota companies. Paul Streitz, President & CEO of Advanced Lighting in Sauk Centre said, "Each and every one of Advanced Lighting's current and future employees owe their jobs to the assistance Minnesota Technology, Inc. has provided." ■

In 2001, the state invested $6.1 million in Minnesota Technology, Inc., for a return of $163 million in economic growth.

Xcel Energy

At Xcel Energy, customer service is a top priority. The company's 3.2 million electric customers and 1.7 million natural gas customers make it the fourth-largest combination electric and natural gas utility in the nation.

Among Xcel Energy's most significant and successful customer service initiatives is its work to help customers conserve energy and manage its use. Over the past decade, the company has built one of the most aggressive energy conservation efforts in the country. Energy audits, loans, and rebates—along with a wide variety of other conservation programs—allow customers to save money on their energy bills. The programs also enable Xcel Energy to more efficiently manage electric demand. On the hottest days of summer, the company is able to reduce its highest electric demand by as much as 10 percent.

Xcel Energy employees work hard to be energy partners, striving to fully understand the businesses their customers operate and offering innovative programs to help those customers make energy management a competitive advantage. At the University of Minnesota, for example, the company participated in the design of a new building at the College of Architecture through Xcel Energy's Energy Design Assistance Program. Special computer modeling of energy-efficient options for the building will enable the college to reduce energy needs for the building by 35 percent over state building-code standards. In addition, Xcel Energy installed a 72-panel photovoltaic system atop the facility, which will serve the building and provide research opportunities.

To benchmark its customer service, Xcel Energy regularly compares its results with other utilities. In 2002, the company was recognized by the Edison Electric Institute as one of the nation's best overall utilities for providing services to multi-site, national energy customers.

The company also offers customers choice-from how they pay their bills to the type of energy they purchase. Last year, Xcel Energy expanded its WindSource program, which allows customers the opportunity to purchase wind power, a renewable energy source, to Minnesota. The company is one of the

Working with customers is a top priority at Xcel Energy.

largest suppliers of wind energy in the nation and includes other renewable energy sources in its portfolio such as hydropower and biomass.

To improve air quality, Xcel Energy has proposed a $1 billion package of projects to reduce emissions at three of the company's generating plants in the Twin Cities metropolitan area. The proposals include converting two coal-fired plants to natural gas and upgrading emissions control equipment at a third plant. In addition to significantly reducing air emissions, the projects will contribute to regional reliability by increasing the plants' generating capacity.

As an energy partner, Xcel Energy will continue to contribute to the high quality of life enjoyed in the Twin Cities metropolitan area. ■

Xcel Energy employees contribute to the community through mentoring and other efforts such as providing electrical safety demonstrations.

CenterPoint Energy Minnegasco

innesota's largest natural gas distribution company has been a trusted provider of efficient and reliable energy for more than 130 years. The company got its start in 1870, when it began lighting the streets of Minneapolis with gas. Today, CenterPoint Energy Minnegasco, headquartered in downtown Minneapolis, serves more than 700,000 residential and business customers in more than 240 Minnesota communities.

The company is not only a trusted supplier of dependable, low-cost natural gas, it also provides year-round gas service installations, online products and service on its Web site, and information promoting safety and efficiency.

CenterPoint Energy Minnegasco actively seeks industry-wide solutions to energy conservation and maintains environmental stewardship as a primary company goal. It has helped many companies, school districts, and other organizations build for energy efficiency by providing solutions-oriented expertise and advice, and conservation improvement rebates to offset some of the costs of installing energy efficient natural gas equipment.

The company has also worked with the state legislature and other stakeholders on energy policy and technological innovations to help Minnesota meet its long-term energy needs. In recent years, CenterPoint Energy Minnegasco has partnered with electric utilities and other customers to develop cost-effective methods of using natural gas to produce electricity. The Black Dog plant in Burnsville uses natural gas to produce electricity that is distributed throughout the Twin Cities, offering substantial benefits in terms of air emissions, energy efficiency, and overall energy reliability. In Chaska,

CenterPoint Energy Minnegasco provides safe, dependable, year-round installation of new natural gas mains and service lines to meet the energy needs of growing Minnesota communities.

the Minnesota River Station does the same for Chaska and seven neighboring cities, providing an economical source of power during peak periods of high summer demand. The company is also developing Distributed Generation applications with many business customers who will use the generated electricity "on-site" at their own facilities.

CenterPoint Energy Minnegasco is committed to the ongoing growth and vitality of the communities it serves. The company sponsored the annual Minneapolis Aquatennial Torchlight Parade in 2001 and 2002, and has supported many other events that contribute to the health and vitality of the city. Many of CenterPoint Energy Minnegasco's 1,500 employees and their families are very active in the community, contributing volunteer hours and financial assistance to programs such as the United Way, Habitat for Humanity, The Salvation Army, Minnesota FoodShare, and the Boys and Girls Clubs of Minneapolis.

President and Chief Operating Officer, Gary Cerny, says CenterPoint Energy Minnegasco will play an important role in providing its customers information about new energy solutions, pricing, and supply portfolio strategies, as well as more conservation-based products and services.

"We'll continue to grow," he says, "providing value and innovation to help our customers become more energy efficient and productive." CenterPoint Energy Minnegasco—always there. ∎

CenterPoint Energy Minnegasco's construction and service vehicles are a sign of safe and reliable service throughout more than 240 Minnesota communities the company serves.

Minnesota Sports & Entertainment

*I*t was with great enthusiasm that dedicated sports fans welcomed once again a professional hockey club in Minnesota. The National Hockey League's Minnesota Wild ventured onto the ice for its first season in 2000. The team and the fans owe this major league accomplishment to the persevering efforts of Governor Arne Carlson, Saint Paul Mayor Norm Coleman, numerous public officials, and Minnesota Sports & Entertainment (MSE), composed of dedicated hockey fans and investors, headed by majority owner, Robert Naegele, Jr.

MSE's foundations were rooted in bringing NHL hockey back to the state of Minnesota after a seven-year absence. In 1997, the investor group was awarded an NHL expansion franchise for the City of Saint Paul. MSE has since grown into an aspiring regional sports and entertainment company that has expanded its business operations.

While the Minnesota Wild NHL franchise is the centerpiece of the business enterprise, MSE also owns the historic Minnesota Club building, now called 317 on Rice Park, which serves as its home offices, and the Saint Paul Arena Company, LLC, which operates Touchstone Energy Place, Roy Wilkins Auditorium, and the new state-of-the-art Xcel Energy Center, home of the Minnesota Wild. This commanding facility in the heart of downtown Saint Paul, is the Upper Midwest's premier meeting, entertainment, and sports venue.

Saint Paul's long history as a meeting place and commercial crossroads along the Mississippi River inspired the RiverCentre complex. Its all-glass exterior offers commanding views of the river and creates a distinguished identity that welcomes visitors. Xcel Energy Center, which was built specifically for the Minnesota Wild, is the newest addition to RiverCentre which already boasts Touchstone Energy Place and Roy Wilkins Auditorium. The 650,000-square-foot arena is not only host to

State-of-the-art Xcel Energy Center. Photo by Cory Schubert

the world's most talented hockey players, but a premier facility for concerts, entertainment events, and family shows.

MSE also owns a majority interest in Wildside Caterers, the result of a joint venture with Morrissey Hospitality Companies. Wildside Caterers is the exclusive caterer for the Xcel Energy Center and Touchstone Energy Place, and a leader in premium food and beverage services for weddings, holidays, and other entertainment events.

Saint Paul has built a reputation as a primary source of sports and entertainment in Minnesota with Xcel Energy Center, RiverCentre, the renowned Ordway Center for Performing Arts, the new Science Museum of Minnesota, and historic and elegant buildings, such as the St. Paul Hotel and 317 on Rice Park. Thousands of visitors come to the city from all over Minnesota, neighboring states, and Canada.

MSE is dedicated to delivering the best of Saint Paul, a city that thrives on an intimate scale, but is animated by its access to the energy and opportunity of the greater Twin Cities metropolitan area. ■

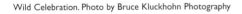

Wild Celebration. Photo by Bruce Kluckhohn Photography

Enterprise Index

Allianz Life Insurance Company of North America
5701 Golden Hills Drive
Minneapolis, Minnesota 55416
Phone: 763-765-6500
www.allianzlife.com
Pages 94-97

Augsburg College
2211 Riverside Avenue
Minneapolis, Minnesota 55454
Phone: 612-330-1001
            800-788-5678
Fax: 612-330-1590
E-mail: admissions@augsburg.edu
www.augsburg.edu
Pages 86-89

Candlewood Suites
351 West 77th Street
Richfield, Minnesota 55423
Phone: 612-869-7704
Fax: 612-869-7383
E-mail: candl372@candlewoodsuites.com
www.candlewoodsuites.com
Page 102

Carlson Companies
701 Carlson Parkway
Mail Stop 8212
Minnetonka, Minnesota 55305
Phone: 763-212-5000
Fax: 763-212-2219
E-mail: smacalus@carlson.com
www.carlson.com
Page 101

CenterPoint Energy Minnegasco
800 LaSalle Avenue
Minneapolis, Minnesota 55402
Phone: 612-372-4664
www.minnegasco.centerpointenergy.com
Page 106

Diversified Equities Corporation
114 Southeast 5th Street, # 127
Minneapolis, Minnesota 55401
Phone: 612-378-1085
Fax: 612-378-1246
E-mail: diversifiedequitiescorp@msn.com
Page 103

Fredrikson & Byron, P.A.
4000 Pillsbury Center
200 South Sixth Street
Minneapolis, Minnesota 55402-1425
Phone: 612-492-7000
Fax: 612-492-7077
www.fredlaw.com
Page 100

Mall of America
60 East Broadway
Bloomington, Minnesota 55425
Phone: 952-883-8800
www.mallofamerica.com
Pages 90-93

Minneapolis Regional Chamber of Commerce
81 South Ninth Street, Suite 200
Minneapolis, Minnesota 55402-3223
Phone: 612-370-9100
Fax: 612-370-9195
E-mail: info@minneapolischamber.org
www.minneapolischamber.org
Pages 98-99

Minnesota Sports & Entertainment
317 Washington Street
Saint Paul, Minnesota 55102
Phone: 651-602-6000
Fax: 651-222-1055
www.wild.com
Page 107

Minnesota Technology, Inc.
111 Third Avenue South, #400
Minneapolis, Minnesota 55401
Phone: 612-373-2900
Fax: 612-373-2901
E-mail: dcumming@mntech.org
www.minnesotatechnology.org
Page 104

PricewaterhouseCoopers
650 Third Avenue South, Suite 1300
Minneapolis, Minnesota 55402
Phone: 612-596-6000
Fax: 612-373-7160
E-mail: karen.r.johnson@us.pwcglobal.com
www.pwcglobal.com
Pages 82-85

Xcel Energy
800 Nicollet Mall
Minneapolis, Minnesota 55402
Phone: 800-328-8226
www.xcelenergy.com
Page 105

Index